GW00373020

Transport Statistics Report

Vehicle Licensing Statistics 1996

Motor vehicles currently licensed, new registrations, goods vehicle statistics.

Published June 1997

London: The Stationery Office

Crown copyright 1997
Published with the permission of the Department of Transport on behalf of the controller of Her Majesty's Stationery Office.
First published June 1997
ISBN 0 11 551928 9

Brief extracts from this publication may be reproduced provided the source is fully acknowledged. Proposals for reproduction of larger extracts should be addressed to the Copyright Unit, Her Majesty's Stationery Office, St Clements House, 2-16 Colegate, Norwich, NR3 1BQ.

Government Statistical Service

A service of statistical information and advice is provided to the Government by specialist staff employed in individual departments. Statistics are made generally available through their publications and further information and advice on them can be obtained from the Departments concerned.

Enquiries about the contents of this publication should be made to:

Department of Transport
Strategy and Analysis Unit
Statistics branch TSA2
Zone 1/34
Great Minster House
76 Marsham Street
London
SW1P 4DR
Telephone 0171 271 3740

25 JUN 1997

Oxfordshire County Libraries

Date 12·6·97

Class No. 0/629· 22007
TRA

NOT FOR LOAN

Perm.

Produced from camera ready copy supplied by the Department of Transport.

The price of this publication has been set to contribute to the preparation costs incurred at the Department of Transport.

CONTENTS   PAGE

Motor vehicles registered for the first time - historic series

Goods vehicles statistics

Introduction

This is the 5th edition of "Vehicle Licensing Statistics" and is published in a similar basic format to the 1995 edition, with 24 tables, accompanied by commentary and charts. However, this report contains several important changes from the 1995 edition and these are described below.

Table 6, which shows the number of licensed and unlicensed vehicles on DVLA files at the end of the year, has been enhanced to provide information on how recently unlicensed vehicles have been licensed for use on public roads. It has also been expanded to cover buses, motorcycles and goods vehicles in addition to cars.

Table 8, which shows vehicles stocks by region, has been brought up to date by the use of the most recently available post code directory, to allow vehicle stocks to be estimated for the new local authorities in Scotland and Wales, and for those unitary authorities that have been created so far in England. Similar changes have been made in Table 24, which deals with goods vehicle stocks by region.

The small section on international comparisons has been dropped. This topic produced few enquiries, and the enquiry almost invariably resulted in further consultation of the Department's more specialised publications. Anyone interested in such comparisons is recommended to go directly to the "International Comparisons of Transport Statistics" report, or other specialist statistics publications.

Tables 21 and 23 which give details on goods vehicle body types have been reduced to cover only rigid lorries. Earlier editions attempted to provide the same information for articulated vehicles, but this has proved to be of limited value. There are roughly two articulated vehicle trailers to every tractor unit and a majority of trailers are described only as "goods" body type or "not known". So little useful information on the trailer is available, with the result that where numbers are given for a specific body type they become potentially misleading.

This report is intended to be a comprehensive, relevant and detailed compendium of vehicle licensing statistics. Any suggestions on improvements or additional tables that readers might find useful should be directed to the contact point on the inner front cover.

Derek Jones
Statistician
Department of Transport
Statistics Branch TSA2

May 1997

Commentary and charts

Licensed vehicle stock 1986-1996

- The **total vehicle stock in Great Britain** at the end of 1996 was estimated to be 26.30 million vehicles, of which 22.24 million vehicles, or about 85%, were motorcars. The next most numerous vehicle group by body type was light goods vehicles with a stock of over 2.00 million vehicles, or roughly 7.6% of the total.

- The **remainder of the stock** is made up of 739,000 motorcycles; 555,000 other goods vehicles; 286,000 agricultural tractors; 158,000 buses and coaches; 30,000 three wheelers; 34,000 custom built taxis; and 263,000 other assorted vehicle types. Note that a vehicle's body type is not always a reliable guide to its taxation class, for example, of the above 158,000 buses about half are licensed for public use, the bulk of the remainder being minibuses taxed for private use.

- The final group of 263,000 other assorted vehicle types includes emergency service vehicles such as fire engines and ambulances, road repair vehicles such as road surfacers, road surface strippers, bulldozers, tar sprayers, road rollers and line painters, road maintenance vehicles such as street cleansing, snow ploughs and gritting lorries and various types of construction vehicles, cranes, shovels, diggers and excavators.

- With due allowance for the change in census method in 1992, the **total stock of vehicles has grown** by an estimated 22.5% between the end of 1986 and the end of 1996; a rate equivalent to 2.05% per annum. Growth was lower in the early 1990s although nearly 3.7% between 1995 and 1996. Since the end of 1991, the estimated total growth in vehicle stock is 8.4%; a rate equivalent to 1.63% per annum.

- **Growth in motorcar stock** totalled 29.2% between 1986 and 1996, equivalent to 2.60% per annum, and totalled 11.0% between 1991 and 1996 equivalent to 2.10% per annum..

- The stock of vehicles with **goods body types** remained relatively constant between 1986 and 1987, grew by about 6.0% between the end of 1987 and the end of 1989, and has since declined. The stock at the end of 1996 was 555,000 vehicles, an estimated overall reduction of 11.5% since 1986, and a reduction of 16.8% since the 1989 peak.

- Total **motorcycle stocks** have declined considerably over the last ten years, by an estimated 37% in total, a rate equivalent to 4.5% fewer vehicles per year, but **grew by 5.3%** between the end of 1995 and 1996

2

Licensed vehicle stock 1986-1996: By body type

All vehicles

millions

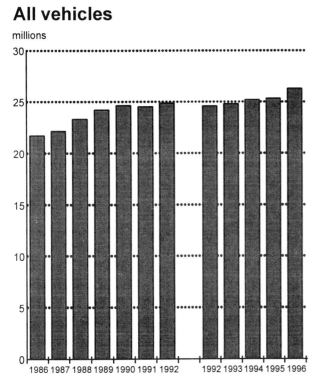

Motorcars

millions

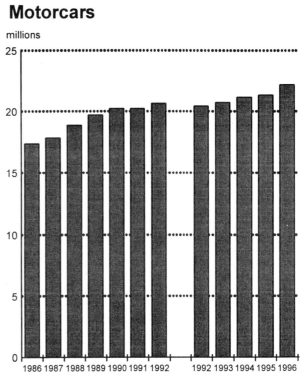

Goods vehicles

thousands

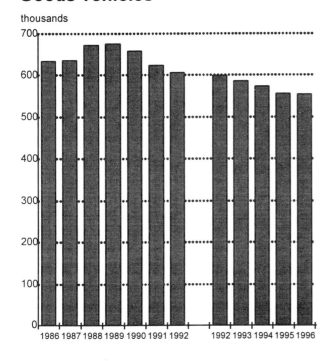

Motorcycles

thousands

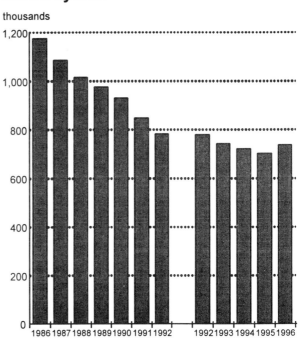

Source: 1985-1992 DVLA Annual Vehicle Census
Source: 1992-1995 DOT Vehicle Information Database

Vehicles registered for the first time 1986 to 1996

- In the past ten years, **new vehicle registrations** have ranged between a maximum of 2.83 million vehicles in 1989 and a minimum of 1.90 million vehicles in 1992. Registrations in 1996, at 2.41 million, were 4.3% higher than the figure for the previous year, and 3.3% above the 1986 total.

- **Registrations of new motorcars** followed a similar pattern, with a maximum of 2.30 million cars in 1989 and a minimum of 1.60 million cars in both 1991 and 1992. Registrations in 1996, at 2.02 million, were 4.1% higher than in 1995. Between 1986 and 1996 the proportion of new vehicles registered to a keeper with a company title has increased from 46% to 52%, while the residue, registered to private keepers has reduced by the corresponding amount. Most of the increase occurred between 1986 and 1988, and since 1988 company registrations have been fairly steady at between 51% and 53%.

- **Since the end of 1986** a total of 23.33 million new vehicles have been registered, while stocks have grown by an estimated 4.88 million. For cars, 19.37 million new cars have been registered, while stocks have grown by an estimated 5.09 million. So roughly 4 in every 5 new vehicles, and roughly 3 in every 4 new cars have replaced existing stocks rather than added to the vehicle population.

- New vehicles registered in **goods vehicle taxation classes** also reached their maximum in 1989 with 65 thousand new registrations, but the minimum was in 1991 with 29 thousand new registrations. The relative gap between these high and low points was much greater than for other vehicle types. Registrations in 1996 at 45.5 thousand vehicles were 5.2% lower than in 1995, 11.5% below the 1986 figure and 29.5% below the 1989 peak.

- Registrations of **new motorcycles** have varied from a high of 106.4 thousand in 1986 to a low of 58.4 thousand in 1993. Numbers have increased each year since 1993, so that the 89.6 thousand registered in 1996 was 30% above the 1995 figure and 53% above the 1993 low.

4

Vehicles registered for the first time: 1986-96

All vehicles

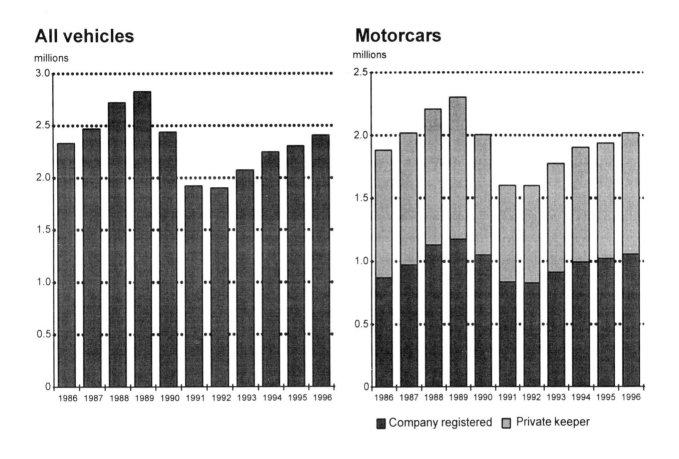

Motorcars

Vehicles in goods tax classes

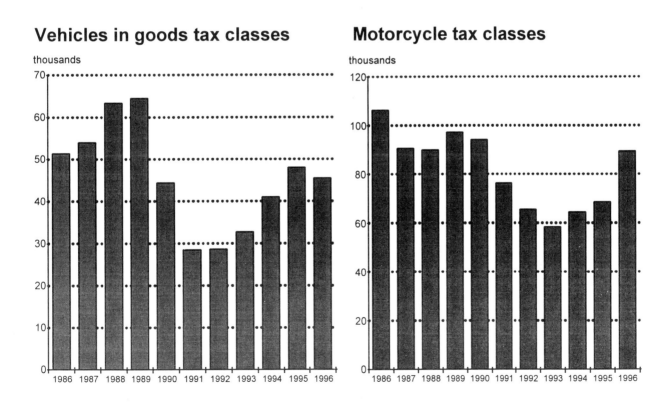

Motorcycle tax classes

Vehicle details: 1985 and 1996 compared

- The taxation group "hackney" for public transport vehicles, which covered both taxis and buses and coaches, was abolished from end of June 1995, and replaced with a new **"bus" taxation group** covering only vehicles with more than 8 seats.

- Comparisons between 1986 and 1996 for vehicles with 8 or fewer seats are not meaningful, and only vehicles with 9 or more are included in the graphs on the opposite page. The group having 9 to 32 seats, which includes minibuses and smaller buses and coaches has increased from roughly 18% to 32% of bus stocks, while the proportion of larger buses and coaches, that is with 48 or more seats has declined from 70% to 57% of stocks.

- The greatest change in the composition of **goods vehicle stock** between 1986 and 1996 has been the marked increase in the proportion of vehicles in the gross weight range from 33 to 38 tonnes, resulting from changes in regulations introduced in May 1983 which increased the maximum gross vehicle weight limit from 32.5 tonnes to 38 tonnes. This increase, and a slight increase in the proportion of lorries in the gross weight range up to 7.5 tonnes (vehicles which can be driven on an ordinary driving licence) is mirrored by a general fall in the proportion of general goods vehicles in other weight ranges.

- As the section on licensed stock showed, the **overall stock of motorcycles** has declined by 37% between 1986 and 1996. Accompanying this change in numbers has been a marked upward shift in the average engine capacity of bikes in use. The proportion having engine capacities up to 50 cc's has fallen by about 20 percentage points, whereas the proportion with capacities over 500 cc's has not only increased from less than 10% to over 35% of licensed stock, but has also doubled in absolute terms from 98,000 to 223,000 bikes.

- **Vehicles subject to one or more forms of exemption** of vehicle excise duty have increased from 721,000 in 1986 to 1,424,000 in 1996. At the end of 1996 278,000 of these vehicles qualified for exemption under the "older than 25 years" rule introduced in the November 1995 budget. The largest single group of exempt vehicles are those owned by disabled drivers, which make up 57% of the 1996 total compared with 37% of the total in 1985. Crown vehicles have more than halved from 39,000 to 15,000 over the ten year period. Exempt vehicles overall have increased from 3.3% of total stock to 5.4% of total licensed stock between 1986 and 1996.

Vehicle details: 1986 and 1996 compared

Public transport vehicles

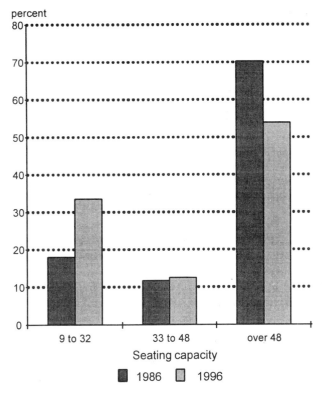

percent

Seating capacity

■ 1986 ▨ 1996

General goods vehicles[1]

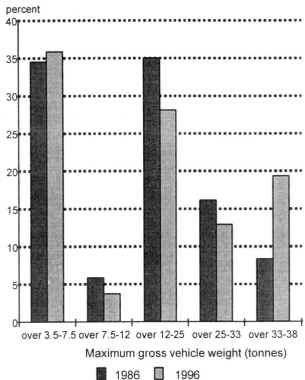

percent

Maximum gross vehicle weight (tonnes)

■ 1986 ▨ 1996

1. 1986 data excludes Farmers goods vehicles. This classification was abolished in July 1995. These vehicles were classified as general goods vehicles on renewal of the licence.

Motorcycles, scooters and mopeds

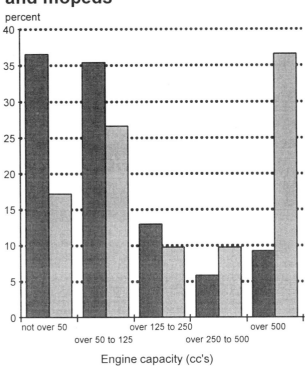

percent

Engine capacity (cc's)

Crown, disabled and other vehicles exempt from duty

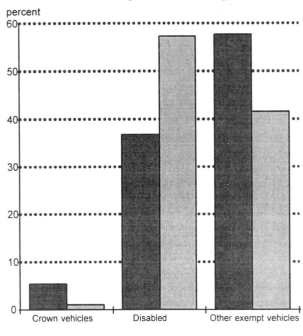

percent

Vehicle type

Current vehicle stock: Year of first registration

- Very few vehicles are not new when first registered. For all practical purposes therefore the **year of first registration** can be used to monitor the age of any sample of vehicles. For example, vehicles first registered in 1996 will, in general, be not more than one year old by the end of that year, vehicles first registered in 1995 not more than two years old at the end of 1996, etc. etc.

- The age profile of most vehicles types reflects the peak in new registration which occurred in 1989. Despite wastage, the group of PLG **motorcars** registered in 1989 remains the largest at almost 9.4% of licensed stock. Of currently licensed motorcars over 16% are not more than two years old, but roughly 1% were registered before 1980, and are now at least 17 years old.

- Among the common vehicle types, **public transport vehicles** (vehicles with more than 8 seats only) have the largest group of old vehicles, with about 13% registered before 1980, and now at least 17 years old. Other age groups are roughly evenly distributed, albeit with some peaking in the 1986 to 1990 period. Around 15% of current vehicles were registered in 1995 and 19996 and were therefore not more than two years old at the end of 1996.

- Although **motorcycles** are generally among the most short lived of all vehicles, older bikes were registered in substantially greater numbers than in recent years. For example, in 1980 and 1981 a combined total of over 570,000 new bikes were registered compared with a combined total of 158,500 in 1995 and 1996. Of currently licensed motobikes, around 20% are not more than two years old, but, despite wastage, substantial numbers of older bikes remain in the currently licensed stock so that even vehicles registered before 1980 still make up about 7% of current stocks.

- Currently licensed **goods vehicles** show a marked peak in 1988 and 1989 when registrations were very high. The proportion of vehicles registered in these two years forming roughly 9% and 10% respectively of currently licensed stock. Under 1% of goods vehicles were registered before 1980, and over 22% were registered within the last two years. Goods vehicles over 38 tonnes gross weight can only be used for combined transport operations and almost all registrations over this weight have been in 1995 and 1996.

Current vehicle stock: Year of 1st registration

Motorcars: PLG taxation group

percent

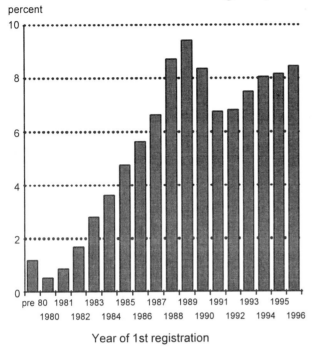

Year of 1st registration

Public transport vehicles: 9 or more seats

percent

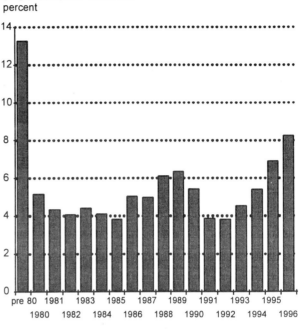

Year of 1st registration

General goods vehicles

percent

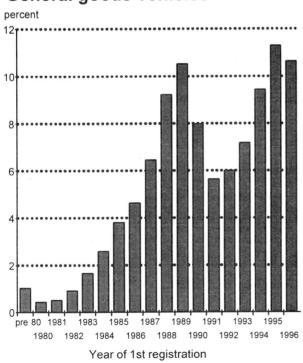

Year of 1st registration

Motorcycles, scooters and mopeds

percent

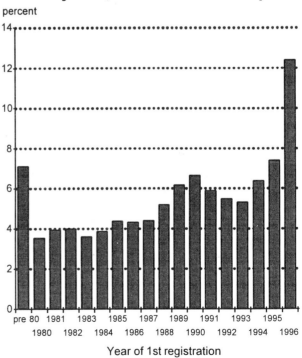

Year of 1st registration

Goods vehicle stock 1996

-       Tables 15 onwards in this report give details of the currently licensed "**goods vehicle stock**". Although tabulations giving information on vehicles in goods vehicle taxation classes, and having goods vehicle construction are useful, they have some disadvantages.

-       For example, in earlier years some vehicles may be in goods vehicle taxation groups and weigh less than 3,500 kgs, which would normally result in being taxed in the Private and Light Goods group. Moreover, some heavy goods vehicles may be taxed in other groups.

-       Tables 15 onwards give statistics for a carefully defined set of currently licensed goods vehicles, all of which exceed 3,500 kgs maximum gross vehicle weight. The vehicles included are all those in taxation classes 1 and 2 (the main heavy goods vehicle taxation groups) class 16 - small island goods vehicles, plus vehicles with goods vehicle body types in electric taxation groups, crown vehicles and other exempt classes provided they have goods vehicle body types.

-       The goods vehicle stock, defined in this way, stood at 421,000 vehicles at the end of 1996, of which 311,000 were rigid vehicles and 110,000 articulated. This is a slight rise of 0.7% on 1995 and is the third year to show an increase following a period of decline from the 1989 peak of 478,000 vehicles.

-       Many goods vehicles are constructed to maximise the amount of goods that can be carried within regulations and taxation bands. **Rigid 2 axle goods vehicles** cannot exceed 17 tonnes, **rigid 3 axle goods vehicles** cannot exceed 24.39 tonnes and rigid 4 axle goods cannot exceed 30.49 tonnes. The maximum weight for **4 axle articulated** goods vehicles is 33 tonnes, and for **5 axle articulated** goods vehicles 38 tonnes. **Articulated vehicles with 6 axles** are permitted a maximum gross vehicle weight of up to 44 tonnes provided they are engaged in Combined Transport operations only. The maximum weight vehicle that can be driven on an ordinary driving license in 7.5 tonnes.

-       Two axle vehicles remain the most common form of rigid lorry. Two axle articulated tractor units outnumber 3 axle units by more than two to one. Most articulated tractors are licensed to pull either 3 axle trailers, or any axle trailer configuration. Articulated vehicle **trailers** do not need to be registered with DVLA and are not subject to vehicle excise duty. They are, however, subject to Vehicle Inspectorate roadworthiness tests, and from this source, the total stock in 1995 is estimated at roughly 227,000 trailers.

Goods vehicle stock 1996: Weight & axle details

Rigid vehicles

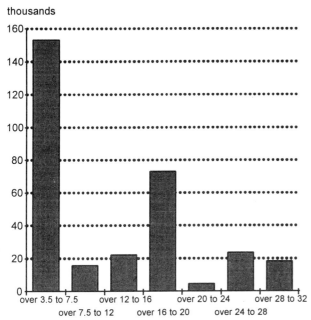

thousands

Maximum gross weight (tonnes)

Articulated vehicles

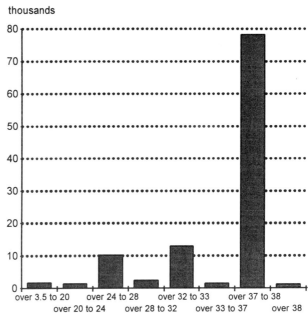

thousands

Maximum gross weight (tonnes)

Rigid vehicles

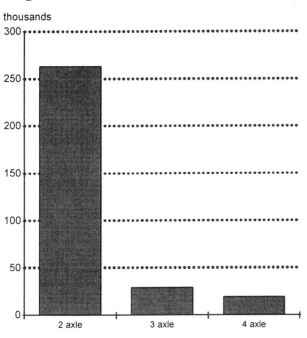

thousands

Axle configuration

Articulated vehicles

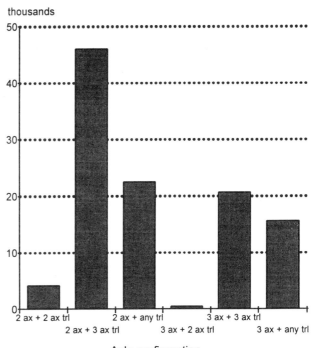

thousands

Axle configuration

11

Currently licensed motorcars: Vehicle details

-       At the end of 1996 there were some 22.24 million vehicles with **car body** types licensed to use GB roads. Of these, an overwhelming majority, 21.17 million cars, were taxed within the private and light goods taxation group. Most of the rest were taxed within the group of exempt vehicles, claiming exemption in the disabled driver category, but since November 1995 some 0.28 million are claiming exemption for being more than 25 years old.

-       The title code of the **registered vehicle keeper** showed that 2.28 million cars, or 10.3% of the total, were registered as company owned.

-       At the end of 1996, some 9.8% of currently licensed motorcars were **diesel** propelled, though just under 8% of vehicles registered to private keepers are diesel propelled vehicles, compared with the 26% of cars registered to companies that are diesel propelled.

-       However, companies tend to own and use newer cars than private keepers. This difference may fall as time passes, and increasing numbers of diesel driven company cars come onto the second hand market. Modern cars are almost exclusively propelled by diesel or petrol, only 0.1% being electrically or otherwise propelled.

-       The **engine capacity** of petrol driven motorcars is, on average, lower than that for diesel driven cars. Only 0.2% of diesel driven cars have engines smaller than 1200 cc's, whereas 9.1% of petrol driven cars have engine capacities less than 1000 cc's. Nevertheless, diesel cars have better fuel consumption figures (that is more miles per gallon of fuel) than petrol driven cars.

-       In other espects, diesel powered cars produce lower emissions of carbon monoxide and hydrocarbons than petrol powered cars, but much higher emissions of particulates (smoke). Diesel cars tend to emit more oxides of nitrogen than petrol cars with three way catalytic converters but less than petrol cars without converters.

Currently licensed motorcars: Vehicle details

Taxation class

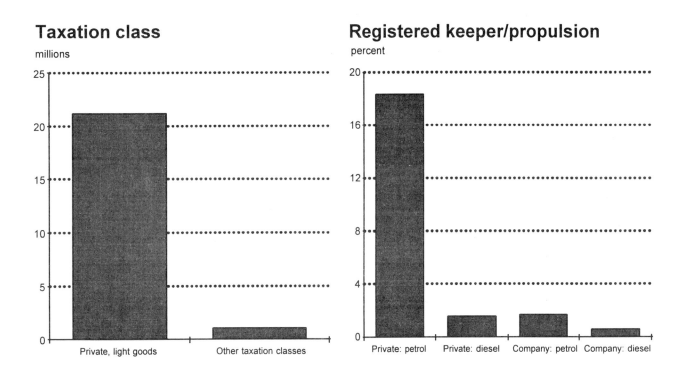

Registered keeper/propulsion

Engine capacity: petrol propulsion

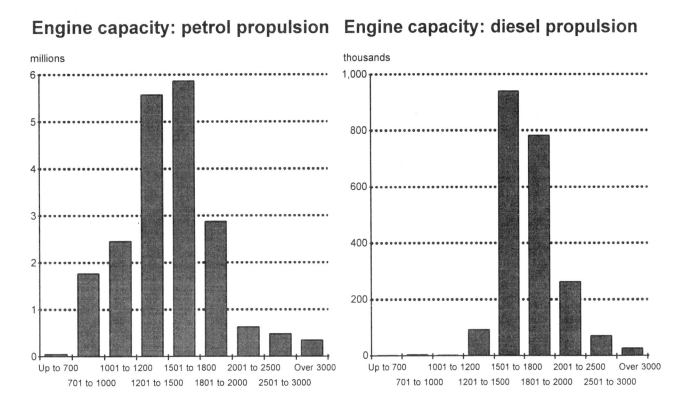

Engine capacity: diesel propulsion

13

Table 1 Motor vehicles currently licensed: by taxation group[1]: 1986-96

Thousands

| | Private and light goods[2] | | | Public transportation | | | | |
| | Body type cars | Other vehicles | Motor cycles scooters and mopeds | Hackney taxation class[3] | *of which:* Bus taxation class[4] | Goods[6] | Special machines/ Special concession[7] | Other vehicles[8] |
Year								
1986	16,981	1,880	1,065	125	68 [5]	484	371	73
1987	17,421	1,952	978	129	71 [5]	485	374	68
1988	18,432	2,096	912	132	73 [5]	502	383	83
1989	19,248	2,199	875	122	73 [5]	505	384	77
1990	19,742	2,247	833	115	73 [5]	482	375	71
1991	19,737	2,215	750	109	72 [5]	449	346	65
1992	20,116	2,228	688	108	73 [5]	437	324	59
1992	19,870	2,198	684	107	72 [5]	432	324	59
1993	20,102	2,187	650	107	73 [5]	428	318	55
1994	20,479	2,192	630	107	75 [5]	434	309	50
1995	20,505	2,217	594	..	74	421	274	44
1996	21,172	2,267	609	..	77	413	254	40

continued

				body type cars in all taxation classes				
					of which:			
	Crown and exempt	Special vehicles group	All vehicles	All body type cars	Company	Diesel	Per cent company	Per cent diesel
Year								
1986	720		21,699	17,389	2,038	245	*11.7*	*1.4*
1987	744		22,152	17,856	2,170	352	*12.2*	*2.0*
1988	761		23,302	18,888	2,391	418	*12.7*	*2.2*
1989	785		24,196	19,720	2,579	528	*13.0*	*2.7*
1990	807		24,673	20,230	2,613	638	*12.9*	*3.2*
1991	840		24,511	20,253	2,435	751	*12.0*	*3.7*
1992	891		24,851	20,681	2,321	931	*11.2*	*4.5*
1992	903		24,577	20,444	2,272	920	*11.1*	*4.5*
1993	979		24,826	20,755	2,221	1,226	*10.7*	*5.9*
1994	1,030		25,231	21,199	2,197	1,576	*10.4*	*7.4*
1995	1,169	28 [9]	25,369 [10]	21,394	2,231	1,891	*10.4*	*8.8*
1996	1,424	48 [9]	26,302	22,238	2,283	2,182	*10.3*	*9.8*

1 See notes and definitions.
2 For years up to 1990 retrospective counts within these new taxation classes have been estimated.
3 Taxation class 35, Hackney. Public transportation vehicles including taxis: Abolished 30th June 1995
4 Taxation class 34, Buses. Public transportation vehicles with more than 8 seats: Introduced 1st July 1995.
5 Estimated: Retrospective estimates are based on vehicles registrations in tax class 35, with more than 8 seats
6 Until 30th June 1995 included agricultural vans and lorries and showman's goods vehicles licensed to draw trailers. From 1st July 1995 separate taxation groups for farmers and showmen were abolished.
7 The agricultural and special machines taxation group was abolished on 30th June 1995 and replaced by the special concession taxation group from 1st July 1995.
8 Includes crown and exempt vehicles, three wheelers, and others.
9 Special vehicles group: Introduced 1st July 1995.
10 Contains 44,000 vehicles still taxed in abolished taxation classes at the end of 1995.

14

Table 2 Motor vehicles currently licensed: vehicle details: 1986-96[1]

(a) Private and light goods:[2] Body type cars within private and light goods by engine size

Thousands

Over	Not over	1986	1987	1988	1989	1990	1991	1992	1992	1993	1994	1995	1996
	700 cc	120	114	108	99	90	79	71	70	62	54	46	42
700 cc	1,000 cc	1,963	2,022	2,145	2,205	2,215	2,163	2,109	2,084	1,998	1,905	1,757	1,678
1,000 cc	1,200 cc	2,153	2,154	2,201	2,215	2,226	2,198	2,232	2,207	2,227	2,261	2,258	2,327
1,200 cc	1,500 cc	5,115	5,111	5,259	5,361	5,418	5,358	5,411	5,349	5,330	5,337	5,225	5,321
1,500 cc	1,800 cc	4,573	4,850	5,279	5,641	5,872	5,944	6,105	6,025	6,129	6,276	6,345	6,540
1,800 cc	2,000 cc	1,616	1,718	1,920	2,162	2,352	2,465	2,655	2,622	2,841	3,088	3,274	3,550
2,000 cc	2,500 cc	694	710	736	747	744	726	727	719	722	759	791	851
2,500 cc	3,000 cc	445	448	476	501	509	498	496	489	482	486	494	524
3,000 cc		301	294	307	314	315	306	309	305	312	313	315	340
cc not known		1	1	1	1	1	1	-	-	-	-	-	0
All capacities		16,981	17,421	18,432	19,248	19,742	19,740	20,116	19,870	20,102	20,479	20,505	21,172
Other vehicles		1,880	1,952	2,095	2,199	2,247	2,215	2,230	2,198	2,187	2,192	2,217	2,267
All PLG		18,259	19,374	20,528	21,447	21,989	21,952	22,345	22,069	22,289	22,672	22,722	23,439

(b) Motor cycles, scooters and mopeds: by engine size

Thousands

Over	Not over	1986	1987	1988	1989	1990	1991	1992	1992	1993	1994	1995	1996
	50 cc	389	352	312	280	248	207	174	173	147	129	112	105
50 cc	125 cc	377	347	320	303	284	249	221	222	204	187	170	162
125 cc	150 cc	5	4	3	3	3	2	2	2	2	2	1	1
150 cc	200 cc	45	39	34	31	28	24	21	22	19	18	14	13
200 cc	250 cc	88	78	71	68	65	60	55	55	52	50	46	46
250 cc	350 cc	13	13	15	16	16	15	15	15	15	15	12	11
350 cc	500 cc	49	46	45	45	45	42	42	41	42	45	43	48
500 cc		98	99	112	131	146	150	158	155	169	186	196	223
All over 50 cc		676	626	600	595	587	543	514	512	503	502	482	504
All engine sizes		1,065	978	912	875	835	750	688	684	650	630	594	609

(c) Public transport vehicles: by seating capacity

Thousands

Over	Not over	1986	1987	1988	1989	1990	1991	1992	1992	1993	1994	1995	1996
	4 seats	47.0	47.7	46.7	35.3	26.8	21.5	18.1	18.0	15.4	13.3	2.6	
4 seats	8 seats	9.6	10.5	13.0	14.0	15.0	16.1	17.1	17.0	17.9	19.2	5.5	
All 8 seats or less		56.6	58.2	59.7	49.3	42.0	37.6	35.3	35.0	33.4	32.5	8.0	
8 seats	32 seats	12.3	15.3	17.3	18.9	20.0	20.7	21.5	21.4	22.5	23.2	23.5	25.7
32 seats	48 seats	8.0	7.7	7.3	6.7	6.3	6.1	6.4	6.4	6.8	7.8	8.6	9.6
48 seats		48.0	47.9	48.2	47.3	46.2	44.8	44.6	44.4	43.9	43.5	41.6	41.3
All over 8 seats		68.4	70.8	72.8	72.9	72.5	71.5	72.5	72.2	73.3	74.5	73.8	76.6
All capacities		125.0	129.0	132.5	122.2	114.7	109.1	107.8	107.2	106.6	107.0	..	

(d) General goods: by gross weight

Thousands

Over	Not over	1986	1987	1988	1989	1990	1991	1992	1992	1993	1994	1995	1996
3.5 tonnes	7.5 tonnes	141	145	153	157	155	148	143	143	139	139	144	148
7.5 tonnes	12 tonnes	24	22	21	20	18	17	16	16	15	15	15	15
12 tonnes	25 tonnes	143	143	147	146	140	129	124	123	120	118	118	116
25 tonnes	33 tonnes	66	64	65	62	55	49	46	45	47	51	52	53
33 tonnes	38 tonnes	34	41	51	59	61	60	63	62	65	71	76	80
38 tonnes		-	-	-	-	-	-	-	-	-	-	1	1
Gross weight unknown		7	7	7	7	2	1	1	1	-	-	-	
All vehicles		415	422	444	451	432	403	393	389	387	394	406	413

1 The vehicle taxation system was subject to major revisions in 1995.
2 Counts of vehicles in 'Private and light goods' have been estimated up to 1991.

Table 2 (continued)

(e) Farmers' goods: by gross weight/Abolished - vehicles will move to other groups on renewal of tax disk.   Thousands

Over	Not over	1986	1987	1988	1989	1990	1991	1992	1992	1993	1994	1995	1996
	3.5 tonnes	22	21	19	18	20	20	19	19	19	20	7	
3.5 tonnes	7.5 tonnes	8	7	7	7	7	7	7	7	6	6	2	
7.5 tonnes	12 tonnes	2	2	2	2	1	1	1	1	1	1	-	
12 tonnes	25 tonnes	7	6	6	5	4	5	5	5	4	4	2	
25 tonnes	33 tonnes	1	1	1	1	1	1	1	1	1	1	-	
33 tonnes	38 tonnes	-	-	-	-	1	1	1	1	1	1	-	
38 tonnes		-	-	-	-	-	-	-	-	-	-	-	
Gross weight unknown		28	25	23	20	14	12	10	10	8	7	2	
All vehicles		68	62	58	54	48	46	43	43	41	40	15	

(f) Special machines/special concession group (Mainly agricultural tractors and machinery)   Thousands

	1986	1987	1988	1989	1990	1991	1992	1992	1993	1994	1995	1996
Agricultural tractors	244	245	246	241	237	221	209	210	207	202	203	190
Combine harvesters and other agric. machinery	42	42	43	43	44	41	40	40	40	40	44	41
Mowing machines	11	11	12	12	11	8	7	7	7	6	6	6
Electric											16	13
Gritting vehicle											3	3
Snow plough											1	1
Steam vehicles											-	-
All vehicles	371	374	383	384	376	346	324	324	318	309	274	254

(g) Other licensed vehicles   Thousands

	1986	1987	1988	1989	1990	1991	1992	1992	1993	1994	1995	1996
Three wheelers less than 450 kgs	67	62	57	53	48	43	39	39	35	32	29	27
General haulage [3]	6	6	6	5	4	3	2	2	2	2	2	2
Others	-	1	20	20	20	19	18	18	17	15		
Recovery											13	11
All vehicles	73	68	83	77	72	65	59	59	55	50	44	40

(h) Crown and other vehicles exempt from licence duty   Thousands

	1986	1987	1988	1989	1990	1991	1992	1992	1993	1994	1995	1996
Crown vehicles	39	39	38	38	38	36	35	36	34	34	20	15
Other exempt:												
Disabled	265	296	323	353	385	421	477	483	571	643	718	816
Over 25 years old	0	0	0	0	0	0	0	0	0	0	120	278
Others	416	410	399	394	385	383	379	384	374	353	312	314
All other exempt	681	706	722	747	770	804	855	867	945	996	1150	1409
All exempt vehicles	721	744	761	785	808	840	891	903	979	1030	1169	1424

(i) Special vehicles group: Tax class 14 and 15   Thousands

	1986	1987	1988	1989	1990	1991	1992	1992	1993	1994	1995	1996
Special vehicles group											28	48

(j) Other abolished tax groups/Vehicles will transfer to other tax groups on renewal of tax disk.   Thousands

	1986	1987	1988	1989	1990	1991	1992	1992	1993	1994	1995	1996
Digging machines	37	39	42	44	43	40	36	36	35	34	17	
Mobile cranes	9	8	9	9	9	8	7	7	7	6	3	
Works trucks	28	29	32	34	32	29	25	25	23	21	13	

3   Until end June 1995 also included showman's haulage.

Table 3 Motor vehicles currently licensed: by body type: 1986-1996

Thousands

Year	Cars	Taxis [1]	Motor cycles	Three wheelers	Light goods	Goods	Buses and coaches	Agricultural vehicles etc [2]	Other vehicles [3]	All vehicles
1986	17,389	26	1,176	60	1,670	634	149	340	256	21,699
1987	17,856	28	1,086	57	1,732	636	150	340	267	22,152
1988	18,888	29	1,016	54	1,863	671	155	341	286	23,302
1989	19,720	30	976	51	1,956	674	156	334	298	24,196
1990	20,230	32	932	47	1,994	658	157	328	297	24,673
1991	20,253	32	848	43	1,961	624	154	309	287	24,511
1992 [4]	20,681	32	784	40	1,976	606	155	297	280	24,851
1992 [5]	20,444	32	780	40	1,951	600	154	298	280	24,577
1993	20,755	32	744	36	1,943	587	153	294	282	24,826
1994	21,199	32	721	34	1,951	575	154	285	281	25,231
1995	21,394	33	702	31	1,949	556	153	282	268	25,369
1996	22,238	34	739	30	2,000	555	158	286	263	26,302

1 These include only custom built `black cab' design vehicles.

2 Includes various types of harvesters, works trucks, mobile cranes and mowing machines.

3 Examples include ambulances, fire engines, road rollers, road construction vehicles, street cleansing etc etc.

4 For the years up to 1992 estimates are taken from the annual vehicle census based upon DVLA main vehicle file.

5 From 1992 estimates of licensed stock are taken from the Depatment of Transport's Statistics Directorate Vehicle Information Database.

Table 4 Motor vehicles currently licensed 1996: By year of first registration

(a) Private and light goods: Body type cars within private and light goods by engine size · Thousands

Over	Not over	Pre 1980	1980	1981	1982	1983	1984	1985	1986	1987
Petrol cars										
	700 cc	1.5	0.6	1.0	1.8	2.0	2.3	3.5	5.1	5.7
700 cc	1,000 cc	31.6	16.6	39.0	50.9	81.8	103.1	126.2	150.5	171.2
1,000 cc	1,200 cc	34.0	20.6	30.4	61.4	88.2	118.2	134.9	144.4	152.5
1,200 cc	1,500 cc	70.7	34.5	55.2	106.1	176.4	229.0	289.0	334.1	380.6
1,500 cc	1,800 cc	50.3	18.6	32.6	85.7	161.5	214.2	316.1	386.3	462.7
1,800 cc	2,000 cc	22.9	9.9	13.9	31.1	58.5	72.7	101.7	124.6	179.8
2,000 cc	2,500 cc	18.5	8.3	13.0	21.3	31.1	34.3	38.1	47.0	46.2
2,500 cc	3,000 cc	15.9	4.8	6.1	12.9	20.6	21.3	24.6	26.7	30.0
3,000 cc		23.4	5.2	5.7	7.1	9.4	11.2	14.1	13.8	16.0
All petrol cars		268.8	119.2	196.8	378.3	629.4	806.2	1,048.4	1,232.6	1,444.9
Diesel cars										
	700 cc	0.1	0.0	0.0	0.0	0.0	0.0	0.0	0.0	0.0
700 cc	1,000 cc	0.0	0.0	0.0	0.0	0.0	0.3	0.5	0.3	0.3
1,000 cc	1,200 cc	0.0	0.0	0.0	0.0	0.0	0.1	0.1	0.1	0.1
1,200 cc	1,500 cc	0.2	0.1	0.0	0.1	0.1	0.1	0.1	0.1	0.1
1,500 cc	1,800 cc	0.0	0.1	1.1	2.7	3.7	11.7	23.5	33.1	38.0
1,800 cc	2,000 cc	0.2	0.1	0.1	0.1	0.9	2.7	4.8	7.0	16.5
2,000 cc	2,500 cc	1.7	0.6	0.7	1.2	3.6	5.5	6.0	6.9	10.6
2,500 cc	3,000 cc	0.4	0.1	0.1	0.4	0.7	0.7	1.4	1.7	1.4
3,000 cc		1.0	0.3	0.5	0.6	0.6	0.5	0.6	0.6	0.4
All diesel cars		3.5	1.3	2.5	5.1	9.6	21.6	36.9	49.6	67.6
Other car propulsion types		-	-	-	-	-	-	-	-	-
Other vehicles		60.1	16.4	17.9	28.7	48.3	69.0	103.5	138.6	171.5
All PLG		332.4	136.9	217.3	412.1	687.4	896.8	1,188.8	1,420.8	1,684.0

(b) Motor cycles, scooters and mopeds: by engine size · Thousands

Over	Not over	Pre 1980	1980	1981	1982	1983	1984	1985	1986	1987
	50 cc	4.3	2.6	4.2	6.1	5.8	6.6	8.1	7.2	7.0
50 cc	125 cc	8.7	3.8	4.2	6.6	8.4	9.4	10.6	10.5	10.4
125 cc	150 cc	0.3	-	-	-	-	-	-	-	-
150 cc	200 cc	3.3	1.9	2.0	0.9	0.5	0.4	0.4	0.2	0.1
200 cc	250 cc	6.2	5.9	5.6	3.7	1.3	0.8	0.7	0.8	0.9
250 cc	350 cc	0.3	0.2	0.5	0.2	0.3	0.3	0.4	0.8	0.8
350 cc	500 cc	6.0	2.6	2.5	2.4	1.5	1.0	1.3	1.2	1.2
500 cc		13.9	4.5	4.9	4.2	4.3	4.9	5.1	5.6	6.3
All over 50 cc		38.8	18.9	19.7	18.2	16.2	16.8	18.5	19.1	19.7
All engine sizes		43.1	21.5	23.9	24.3	21.9	23.4	26.5	26.3	26.7

(c) Public transport vehicles: by seating capacity · Thousands

Over	Not over	Pre 1980	1980	1981	1982	1983	1984	1985	1986	1987
8 seats	32 seats	0.2	-	0.2	0.2	0.3	0.4	0.8	2.1	2.6
32 seats	48 seats	1.4	0.3	0.2	0.2	0.2	0.1	0.2	0.1	0.1
48 seats		8.5	3.6	2.9	2.8	2.9	2.6	2.0	1.7	1.1
All capacities		10.2	4.0	3.3	3.1	3.4	3.2	2.9	3.9	3.8

Table 4 (continued)

(a) Private and light goods: Body type cars within private and light goods by engine size   Thousands

Over	Not over	1988	1989	1990	1991	1992	1993	1994	1995	1996	All years
Petrol cars											
	700 cc	4.8	3.7	1.7	0.8	0.9	1.2	1.6	1.1	1.0	40.2
700 cc	1,000 cc	197.0	172.7	132.6	89.9	55.7	65.9	67.4	64.5	58.6	1,675.1
1,000 cc	1,200 cc	160.9	171.3	172.3	151.7	174.9	177.1	171.1	188.1	172.7	2,324.8
1,200 cc	1,500 cc	449.5	489.4	447.1	356.7	374.4	368.6	353.6	341.3	379.0	5,235.2
1,500 cc	1,800 cc	539.8	567.8	490.1	397.7	349.2	371.7	378.1	394.1	426.0	5,642.5
1,800 cc	2,000 cc	238.3	301.6	273.0	216.9	222.7	228.5	227.9	219.6	250.4	2,793.9
2,000 cc	2,500 cc	40.2	39.0	30.9	23.7	22.8	27.8	47.9	50.9	53.4	594.6
2,500 cc	3,000 cc	39.6	47.8	38.9	24.2	22.4	21.9	24.5	36.2	35.5	454.0
3,000 cc		22.6	24.1	21.0	15.0	15.4	20.6	23.0	28.4	36.4	312.4
All petrol cars		1,692.6	1,817.3	1,607.6	1,276.5	1,238.5	1,283.3	1,295.2	1,324.3	1,412.9	19,072.6
Diesel cars											
	700 cc	0.1	0.1	0.1	0.1	0.1	0.1	0.2	0.2	0.2	1.3
700 cc	1,000 cc	0.3	0.2	0.2	0.2	0.3	0.2	0.1	0.1	0.1	3.1
1,000 cc	1,200 cc	0.1	0.1	0.1	0.2	0.2	0.2	0.3	0.2	0.2	2.0
1,200 cc	1,500 cc	0.3	2.7	4.4	3.8	7.1	28.3	26.9	8.4	2.3	85.2
1,500 cc	1,800 cc	39.8	48.6	49.2	58.4	80.0	107.7	144.7	147.2	107.4	896.9
1,800 cc	2,000 cc	20.7	30.6	33.7	37.3	60.7	117.5	148.4	129.7	144.8	755.6
2,000 cc	2,500 cc	13.4	12.7	12.2	13.6	17.0	25.6	38.5	45.2	41.1	256.0
2,500 cc	3,000 cc	3.0	3.5	4.1	4.4	3.7	5.0	10.9	13.9	14.5	69.6
3,000 cc		0.6	0.9	0.7	0.6	2.6	4.6	3.9	3.4	3.4	25.7
All diesel cars		78.2	99.4	104.7	118.4	171.7	289.2	373.8	348.2	313.9	2,095.2
Other car propulsion types		-	-	-	-	-	-	1.1	1.4	1.3	4.1
Other vehicles		213.3	230.0	192.4	142.6	142.5	138.3	169.1	186.2	198.6	2,267.1
All PLG		1,984.1	2,146.7	1,904.6	1,537.6	1,552.7	1,710.9	1,839.2	1,860.1	1,926.8	23,439.0

(b) Motor cycles, scooters and mopeds: by engine size   Thousands

Over	Not over	1988	1989	1990	1991	1992	1993	1994	1995	1996	All years
	50 cc	7.2	7.6	7.2	5.3	4.3	3.6	4.4	4.8	8.5	104.8
50 cc	125 cc	11.7	12.9	12.9	9.7	8.4	7.1	7.2	7.7	12.1	162.2
125 cc	150 cc	-	-	-	-	-	-	-	-	-	0.7
150 cc	200 cc	0.4	0.5	0.5	0.4	0.3	0.2	0.3	0.3	0.5	13.2
200 cc	250 cc	1.3	2.1	2.5	1.9	2.0	1.9	2.0	2.3	3.9	45.6
250 cc	350 cc	0.8	0.8	0.8	0.8	0.9	0.8	0.8	0.7	0.9	11.2
350 cc	500 cc	1.2	1.5	1.9	2.2	2.4	2.5	4.0	4.7	8.3	48.1
500 cc		9.0	12.2	14.6	15.5	15.3	16.4	20.2	24.7	41.3	222.9
All over 50 cc		24.4	30.0	33.2	30.6	29.2	28.8	34.5	40.3	67.0	503.8
All engine sizes		31.6	37.6	40.4	35.9	33.4	32.5	38.9	45.1	75.5	608.5

(c) Public transport vehicles: by seating capacity   Thousands

Over	Not over	1988	1989	1990	1991	1992	1993	1994	1995	1996	All years
8 seats	32 seats	2.6	2.3	2.1	1.7	1.4	1.6	2.0	2.2	3.1	25.7
32 seats	48 seats	0.2	0.2	0.4	0.3	0.7	0.8	1.2	1.4	1.4	9.6
48 seats		1.8	2.3	1.7	1.0	0.9	1.0	1.0	1.6	1.9	41.3
All capacities		4.7	4.9	4.2	3.0	2.9	3.5	4.2	5.3	6.3	76.7

Table 4 (continued)

(d) General goods:by gross weight

Thousands

Over	Not over	Pre 1980	1980	1981	1982	1983	1984	1985	1986	1987
3.5 tonnes	7.5 tonnes	2.4	1.0	1.2	1.9	3.1	4.4	6.8	7.9	10.4
7.5 tonnes	12 tonnes	0.5	0.1	0.1	0.2	0.3	0.5	0.6	0.8	1.0
12 tonnes	25 tonnes	1.1	0.6	0.6	1.2	2.4	3.8	5.1	6.3	8.7
25 tonnes	33 tonnes	0.2	0.1	0.1	0.3	0.5	0.8	1.3	1.9	2.8
33 tonnes	38 tonnes	0.1	-	-	0.2	0.5	1.2	1.9	2.3	3.8
38 tonnes		-	-	-	-	-	-	-	-	-
All vehicles		4.3	1.8	2.1	3.8	6.9	10.7	15.7	19.1	26.7

(e) Special machines/Special concession group (Mainly agricultural tractors and machinery)

Thousands

	Pre 1980	1980	1981	1982	1983	1984	1985	1986	1987
Agricultural tractors	30.2	4.4	5.0	6.6	7.7	8.0	8.7	6.7	7.4
Combine harvesters and other agricultural machinery	3.3	0.6	0.6	0.9	1.2	1.4	1.6	1.4	1.6
Mowing machines	-	-	-	-	-	-	-	0.1	0.2
Electric	4.5	0.7	0.7	0.6	0.5	0.4	0.4	0.4	0.5
Gritting vehicle	-	-	-	-	0.1	0.1	0.2	0.2	0.3
Snow plough	0.1	-	-	-	-	-	-	-	-
Steam vehicles	-	-	-	-	-	-	-	-	-
All vehicles	38.2	5.8	6.3	8.2	9.7	10.0	11.0	9.0	10.0

(f) Other licensed vehicles

Thousands

	Pre 1980	1980	1981	1982	1983	1984	1985	1986	1987
Three wheelers less than 450 kgs	5.3	1.4	1.2	2.1	2.1	2.0	1.8	1.9	1.7
General haulage	-	-	-	-	-	-	-	-	0.1
Recovery	1.1	0.4	0.4	0.6	0.7	0.7	0.8	0.8	0.8
All vehicles	6.5	1.8	1.6	2.7	2.8	2.8	2.7	2.8	2.7

(g) Crown and other vehicles exempt from licence duty

Thousands

	Pre 1980	1980	1981	1982	1983	1984	1985	1986	1987
Crown vehicles	4.6	0.3	0.4	0.4	0.3	0.4	0.3	0.4	0.5
Other exempt:									
Disabled	10.7	4.3	7.1	14.4	24.4	30.2	38.0	42.4	46.3
Over 25 years old	235.4	1.7	1.6	1.6	2.3	2.4	1.4	1.4	1.6
Others	185.5	4.2	3.9	4.3	9.5	12.7	5.0	4.5	4.6
All exempt not crown	431.5	10.3	12.5	20.3	36.2	45.3	44.4	48.4	52.5
All exempt vehicles	436.2	10.6	12.9	20.7	36.5	45.7	44.8	48.8	53.0

(h) Special vehicles group: Tax classes 14 and 15

Thousands

	Pre 1980	1980	1981	1982	1983	1984	1985	1986	1987
Special vehicles group	3.5	0.7	0.6	0.8	1.1	1.4	1.5	1.7	2.0

1 The vehicle taxation system was subject to major revisions in 1995.
2 Counts of vehicles in 'Private and light goods' have been estimated up to 1991.
3 Until end June 1995 also included showman's haulage.

Table 4 (continued)

(d) General goods:by gross weight   Thousands

Over	Not over	1988	1989	1990	1991	1992	1993	1994	1995	1996	All years
3.5 tonnes	7.5 tonnes	13.9	15.3	12.5	8.8	9.1	9.6	12.0	14.0	13.5	147.7
7.5 tonnes	12 tonnes	1.3	1.6	1.3	0.9	1.1	1.3	1.0	1.2	1.2	15.2
12 tonnes	25 tonnes	12.3	13.8	10.7	7.0	6.8	7.4	8.4	10.0	9.4	115.7
25 tonnes	33 tonnes	4.4	5.1	3.3	2.5	2.7	4.4	7.5	8.2	7.1	53.2
33 tonnes	38 tonnes	6.2	7.6	5.2	4.0	4.9	7.0	9.8	12.8	12.2	79.7
38 tonnes		-	-	-	-	-	-	0.1	0.5	0.5	1.2
All vehicles		38.1	43.4	33.0	23.3	24.7	29.7	39.0	46.6	43.9	412.8

(e) Special machines/Special concession group (Mainly agricultural tractors and machinery)   Thousands

	1988	1989	1990	1991	1992	1993	1994	1995	1996	All years
Agricultural tractors	9.7	9.6	9.3	8.7	8.7	12.5	13.7	14.8	18.3	190.0
Combine harvesters and other agricultural machinery	2.0	2.2	2.1	2.1	2.3	3.2	4.0	5.4	5.2	41.1
Mowing machines	0.3	0.4	0.5	0.4	0.7	0.7	0.8	0.8	0.9	6.3
Electric	0.5	0.5	0.5	0.5	0.4	0.4	0.4	0.3	0.4	12.6
Gritting vehicle	0.3	0.3	0.2	0.2	0.1	0.2	0.1	0.2	0.1	2.7
Snow plough	-	-	-	0.2	0.1	0.1	-	-	-	1.1
Steam vehicles	-	-	-	-	-	-	-	-	-	-
All vehicles	12.8	12.9	12.7	12.1	12.3	17.1	19.2	21.5	25.0	253.8

(f) Other licensed vehicles   Thousands

	1988	1989	1990	1991	1992	1993	1994	1995	1996	All years
Three wheelers less than 450 kgs	1.7	1.2	1.0	0.1	1.0	0.8	0.7	0.5	0.6	27.1
General haulage	0.1	0.2	0.1	-	-	-	0.1	0.1	-	1.5
Recovery	1.6	0.8	0.6	0.3	0.2	0.2	0.2	0.3	0.3	10.9
All vehicles	3.4	2.2	1.7	0.6	1.3	1.1	1.0	0.9	1.0	39.6

(g) Crown and other vehicles exempt from licence duty   Thousands

	1988	1989	1990	1991	1992	1993	1994	1995	1996	All years
Crown vehicles	0.3	0.5	0.6	0.6	0.8	0.9	1.3	1.0	1.2	14.7
Other exempt:										
Disabled	51.8	53.6	45.4	35.9	35.5	38.9	95.0	113.8	128.4	816.0
Over 25 years old	2.5	3.2	3.6	3.3	2.9	2.5	2.6	2.8	5.6	278.4
Others	1.1	6.5	6.4	6.4	7.1	8.3	11.1	12.5	16.2	314.4
All exempt not crown	55.4	63.3	55.4	45.5	45.4	49.7	108.7	129.1	150.3	1,408.8
All exempt vehicles	60.1	63.8	56.0	46.1	46.2	50.7	110.0	130.1	151.4	1,423.5

(h) Special vehicles group: Tax classes 14 and 15   Thousands

	1988	1989	1990	1991	1992	1993	1994	1995	1996	All years
Special vehicles group	3.2	3.6	2.8	2.1	2.0	2.9	4.6	5.5	7.6	47.7

1 The vehicle taxation system was subject to major revisions in 1995.
2 Counts of vehicles in 'Private and light goods' have been estimated up to 1991.
3 Until end June 1995 also included showman's haulage.

Table 5 Motor vehicles currently licensed 1996: by propulsion type

Thousands

Taxation class:	Petrol	Diesel	Electric	Gas or petrol/gas	Steam	All
Private and light goods	19,941.4	3,492.9	-	4.6	0.1	23,439.0
of which: body type cars	19,072.6	2,095.2	-	4.0	-	21,172.0
Motor cycles scooters and mopeds	608.0	0.5	-	-	-	608.5
Bus	2.1	74.6	-	-	-	76.7
Goods	2.8	409.9	-	-	-	412.8
Special concessionary group	5.8	235.0	12.6	0.2	0.1	253.8
Special vehicles group	0.7	45.6	-	1.3	-	47.7
Other vehicles	27.3	12.2	-	-	-	39.6
Exempt vehicles	1,202.1	213.9	5.6	0.7	1.3	1,423.5
All vehicles	21,790.3	4,485.0	18.3	6.8	1.5	26,301.9
of which:						
Body type cars: All	20,051.6	2,181.6	-	4.1	0.1	22,237.5
Body type cars: Company	1,694.7	587.5	-	1.0	-	2,283.3

Table 6 Vehicles currently licensed and unlicensed:[1] 1996
with details of year of registration and most recent taxation activity.

Thousands

Year of first registration	Licensed on 31/12/96	Unlicensed on 31/12/96	Licensing rate %	of those unlicensed			
				Now retaxed	Last taxed in 1996	Last taxed in 1995	Last taxed in 1994 or before
Motorcars							
Pre 1979	405	9,826	4.0	12	129	139	9,546
1979	89	1,583	5.3	3	52	68	1,460
1980	126	1,370	8.4	3	73	94	1,199
1981	207	1,276	14.0	6	114	136	1,020
1982	399	1,178	25.3	11	184	188	795
1983	666	1,140	36.9	17	254	221	647
1984	861	894	49.1	21	254	182	437
1985	1,123	714	61.1	26	236	137	314
1986	1,324	551	70.6	28	199	97	227
1987	1,558	449	77.6	30	165	73	182
1988	1,823	381	82.7	31	136	57	156
1989	1,971	325	85.9	31	114	47	132
1990	1,760	239	88.1	27	84	34	94
1991	1,433	161	89.9	21	59	24	57
1992	1,449	145	90.9	24	58	25	39
1993	1,615	156	91.2	37	75	19	25
1994	1,771	127	93.3	29	62	20	16
1995	1,793	138	92.9	28	88	22	-
1996	1,865	144	92.8	43	101	-	-
All years	22,238	20,794	51.7	429	2,436	1,584	16,346
Motorcycles							
Pre 1979	29	1,192	2.4	1	21	21	1,149
1979	14	259	5.2	-	9	6	244
1980	22	289	6.9	1	12	9	267
1981	24	251	8.7	1	13	10	227
1982	24	209	10.4	1	13	11	186
1983	22	156	12.3	1	11	9	135
1984	23	125	15.7	-	12	9	104
1985	27	101	20.8	1	12	9	80
1986	26	81	24.4	1	11	8	62
1987	27	65	29.1	1	11	7	47
1988	32	59	34.7	1	12	7	39
1989	38	60	38.3	1	14	8	37
1990	40	54	42.6	1	15	8	31
1991	36	41	46.5	1	13	7	20
1992	33	32	51.1	1	12	6	13
1993	32	25	56.1	1	12	5	8
1994	39	25	61.1	1	13	8	3
1995	45	23	66.2	1	18	4	0
1996	75	14	84.0	1	13	-	0
All years	609	3,066	16.6	14	246	152	2,653

1 On DVLA vehicle files. This excludes vehicles registered in Great Britain and subsequently
  exported but retains scrapped vehicles.

Table 6 (continued)

Year of first registration	Licensed on 31/12/96	Unlicensed on 31/12/96	Licensing rate %	of those unlicensed			
				Now retaxed	Last taxed in 1996	Last taxed in 1995	Last taxed in 1994 or before
Goods							
Pre 1979	3	205	*1.3*	-	1	1	203
1979	2	59	*2.6*	-	1	1	57
1980	2	45	*3.9*	-	1	1	43
1981	2	32	*6.3*	-	1	1	29
1982	4	31	*10.9*	-	2	2	27
1983	7	33	*17.3*	-	3	3	26
1984	11	32	*25.3*	-	4	4	23
1985	16	29	*34.8*	1	5	4	19
1986	19	26	*42.1*	1	6	4	15
1987	27	23	*54.1*	1	6	4	11
1988	38	22	*63.8*	1	7	4	10
1989	43	18	*70.2*	1	7	4	7
1990	33	10	*77.2*	1	4	2	3
1991	23	5	*82.4*	-	3	1	1
1992	25	4	*86.8*	-	2	1	1
1993	30	3	*90.0*	-	2	-	-
1994	39	2	*94.1*	1	1	-	-
1995	47	2	*96.2*	-	1	-	-
1996	44	2	*95.8*	1	1	0	0
All years	413	583	*41.4*	10	59	38	476
Buses							
Pre 1979	7.2	35.5	*17.0*	0.1	2.6	2.1	30.7
1979	2.9	2.8	*50.8*	-	0.6	0.4	1.7
1980	4.0	2.0	*66.9*	0.1	0.4	0.2	1.2
1981	3.3	1.3	*71.8*	0.1	0.3	0.2	0.8
1982	3.1	1.0	*75.1*	-	0.2	0.1	0.6
1983	3.4	0.9	*79.4*	-	0.2	0.1	0.5
1984	3.2	0.8	*80.1*	-	0.2	0.1	0.4
1985	2.9	0.8	*77.9*	-	0.3	0.1	0.4
1986	3.9	1.6	*70.7*	0.1	0.6	0.4	0.6
1987	3.8	1.4	*72.9*	0.1	0.6	0.3	0.4
1988	4.7	0.7	*87.2*	-	0.3	0.1	0.2
1989	4.9	0.6	*88.8*	-	0.3	0.1	0.2
1990	4.2	0.5	*90.2*	-	0.2	0.1	0.1
1991	3.0	0.3	*90.9*	-	0.2	0.1	0.1
1992	2.9	0.2	*93.8*	-	0.1	-	-
1993	3.5	0.2	*93.9*	-	0.1	0.1	-
1994	4.2	0.2	*95.8*	-	0.1	-	-
1995	5.3	0.2	*96.5*	-	0.1	-	0
1996	6.3	0.2	*97.0*	0.1	0.1	0	0
All years	76.7	51.2	*60.0*	0.8	7.7	4.6	38.1

Table 7 Motorcars currently licensed 1996: By year of first registration

Vehicles with car body types in all taxation classes: by cyclinder capacity

Petrol propulsion   Thousands

Over	Not over	Pre 1980	1980	1981	1982	1983	1984	1985	1986	1987
	700 cc	4.6	0.6	1.1	1.9	2.2	2.5	3.6	5.2	5.8
700 cc	1,000 cc	70.5	17.2	40.0	52.4	84.6	106.7	129.7	154.5	175.6
1,000 cc	1,200 cc	77.7	21.2	31.3	63.0	90.6	121.3	138.0	147.8	156.0
1,200 cc	1,500 cc	109.7	35.7	57.2	110.1	183.6	237.9	299.0	345.1	392.0
1,500 cc	1,800 cc	83.4	19.5	34.1	89.5	168.7	223.5	328.5	400.1	477.7
1,800 cc	2,000 cc	33.8	10.4	14.5	32.5	61.3	76.0	105.8	129.2	186.0
2,000 cc	2,500 cc	31.9	9.0	13.8	22.6	32.9	36.2	39.8	48.8	47.8
2,500 cc	3,000 cc	30.3	5.2	6.5	13.7	21.7	22.4	25.8	27.7	31.0
3,000 cc		47.8	5.6	6.1	7.5	10.1	12.0	14.6	14.3	16.5
All capacities [1]		489.7	124.5	204.7	393.3	655.6	838.5	1,084.8	1,272.7	1,488.4

Diesel propulsion

Over	Not over	Pre 1980	1980	1981	1982	1983	1984	1985	1986	1987
	700 cc	0.1	-	-	-	-	-	-	-	-
700 cc	1,000 cc	-	-	-	-	-	0.3	0.5	0.3	0.3
1,000 cc	1,200 cc	-	-	-	-	-	-	-	-	-
1,200 cc	1,500 cc	0.2	0.1	-	-	-	-	-	0.1	0.1
1,500 cc	1,800 cc	-	-	1.1	2.8	3.9	12.1	24.4	34.2	39.2
1,800 cc	2,000 cc	0.2	-	0.1	-	0.9	2.8	4.9	7.2	17.0
2,000 cc	2,500 cc	2.1	0.6	0.7	1.3	3.8	5.8	6.2	7.2	11.1
2,500 cc	3,000 cc	0.4	-	0.1	0.4	0.7	0.7	1.4	1.7	1.4
3,000 cc		1.3	0.3	0.5	0.6	0.6	0.6	0.6	0.6	0.5
All capacities [1]		4.5	1.3	2.7	5.4	10.1	22.5	38.3	51.4	69.8

All propulsion types (includes electricity, steam, gas and petrol/gas)

Over	Not over	Pre 1980	1980	1981	1982	1983	1984	1985	1986	1987
	700 cc	4.8	0.6	1.1	2.0	2.2	2.6	3.7	5.3	5.8
700 cc	1,000 cc	70.5	17.2	40.0	52.4	84.6	107.1	130.2	154.9	175.9
1,000 cc	1,200 cc	77.7	21.2	31.3	63.1	90.7	121.4	138.1	147.8	156.1
1,200 cc	1,500 cc	109.9	35.9	57.3	110.2	183.6	238.0	299.1	345.3	392.2
1,500 cc	1,800 cc	83.5	19.6	35.2	92.3	172.6	235.6	352.9	434.3	516.9
1,800 cc	2,000 cc	34.1	10.5	14.7	32.5	62.2	78.8	110.7	136.4	203.0
2,000 cc	2,500 cc	34.1	9.6	14.6	23.9	36.6	42.0	46.0	55.9	58.8
2,500 cc	3,000 cc	30.7	5.2	6.7	14.2	22.4	23.1	27.2	29.4	32.4
3,000 cc		49.1	5.9	6.6	8.2	10.7	12.5	15.2	14.9	17.0
All capacities [1]		494.3	125.9	207.4	398.7	665.7	861.1	1,123.1	1,324.1	1,558.2

1 Includes unknown and cases where an engine capacity is not applicable.

Table 7 (continued)

Vehicles with car body types in all taxation classes: by cyclinder capacity

Thousands

Over	Not over	1988	1989	1990	1991	1992	1993	1994	1995	1996	All
	700 cc	4.9	3.8	1.7	0.9	0.9	1.3	1.7	1.3	1.2	45.3
700 cc	1,000 cc	202.0	177.0	136.0	92.4	57.3	67.8	73.0	69.8	63.9	1,770.4
1,000 cc	1,200 cc	164.6	175.4	176.1	155.4	179.3	181.8	185.7	209.8	188.7	2,463.8
1,200 cc	1,500 cc	462.6	503.9	460.2	367.3	386.2	382.6	401.0	396.6	442.4	5,573.2
1,500 cc	1,800 cc	556.3	584.5	503.9	408.4	358.6	380.7	390.4	408.0	446.6	5,862.4
1,800 cc	2,000 cc	246.2	310.5	280.4	222.3	227.4	232.4	231.3	222.6	255.7	2,878.3
2,000 cc	2,500 cc	41.3	39.9	31.6	24.2	23.3	28.3	48.6	51.8	54.7	626.5
2,500 cc	3,000 cc	40.8	49.1	40.0	24.9	23.0	22.5	25.2	36.9	36.4	483.0
3,000 cc		23.4	25.3	22.3	15.9	16.1	21.2	23.7	29.1	37.5	348.9
All capacities [1]		1,742.1	1,869.2	1,652.3	1,311.7	1,272.2	1,318.5	1,380.7	1,425.7	1,527.0	20,051.6

Diesel propulsion   Thousands

Over	Not over	1988	1989	1990	1991	1992	1993	1994	1995	1996	All
	700 cc	-	-	-	-	-	0.1	0.2	0.2	0.2	1.5
700 cc	1,000 cc	0.3	0.2	0.2	0.2	0.3	0.2	0.1	0.1	-	3.3
1,000 cc	1,200 cc	0.1	0.2	0.1	0.2	0.2	0.2	0.3	0.2	0.2	2.1
1,200 cc	1,500 cc	0.3	2.8	4.5	3.9	7.3	29.1	31.3	9.3	2.4	91.7
1,500 cc	1,800 cc	40.8	49.9	50.4	59.8	82.2	110.6	150.3	159.3	119.2	940.6
1,800 cc	2,000 cc	21.4	31.5	34.6	38.4	62.5	120.3	152.5	132.9	154.5	782.0
2,000 cc	2,500 cc	13.8	13.1	12.5	13.9	17.3	26.0	39.0	46.0	42.0	262.5
2,500 cc	3,000 cc	3.0	3.6	4.2	4.5	3.8	5.1	11.1	14.1	14.7	71.1
3,000 cc		0.7	0.9	0.7	0.6	2.6	4.6	4.0	3.5	3.5 .	26.8
All capacities [1]		80.6	102.2	107.3	121.5	176.3	296.4	388.8	365.7	336.9	2,181.6

All propulsion types (includes electricity, steam, gas and petrol/gas)   Thousands

Over	Not over	1988	1989	1990	1991	1992	1993	1994	1995	1996	All
	700 cc	5.0	3.9	1.8	1.0	1.0	1.4	1.9	1.4	1.4	46.9
700 cc	1,000 cc	202.3	177.2	136.2	92.6	57.6	68.0	73.2	69.9	64.0	1,773.7
1,000 cc	1,200 cc	164.8	175.5	176.3	155.6	179.6	182.0	186.0	210.1	188.9	2,466.0
1,200 cc	1,500 cc	462.9	506.7	464.7	371.2	393.5	411.7	432.3	406.4	444.9	5,665.6
1,500 cc	1,800 cc	597.2	634.4	554.4	468.2	440.8	491.3	540.9	567.5	565.9	6,803.4
1,800 cc	2,000 cc	267.5	342.0	315.0	260.7	289.9	352.7	383.9	355.6	410.3	3,660.4
2,000 cc	2,500 cc	55.1	53.0	44.2	38.2	40.6	54.4	87.6	97.8	96.7	889.1
2,500 cc	3,000 cc	43.8	52.7	44.1	29.3	26.8	27.7	36.6	51.1	51.0	554.4
3,000 cc		24.1	26.2	23.0	16.6	18.7	25.9	28.3	33.2	42.0	378.0
All capacities [1]		1,822.7	1,971.5	1,759.7	1,433.2	1,448.5	1,615.0	1,770.6	1,792.9	1,865.2	22,237.5

Table 8 Motor vehicles currently licensed: by taxation group: region: 1996

Thousands

Country/region/local authority	Private and light goods		Motor cycles scooters and mopeds	Public transport vehicles	Goods	Special concession
	Body type cars	Other vehicles				
Great Britain	21,172.0	2,267.1	608.5	76.7	412.8	253.8
Vehicle Under Disposal	369.5	45.0	18.3	0.7	5.2	4.1
County Uncoded	81.1	14.6	1.9	0.4	3.7	3.9
England	18,174.5	1,934.9	540.8	61.7	353.7	197.2
Northern Region	907.0	90.3	19.7	4.6	18.1	15.5
Cleveland	158.3	14.5	3.5	0.5	2.7	1.1
Hartlepool UA	22.6	2.1	0.4	0.1	0.3	0.1
Redcar & Cleveland UA	43.8	3.4	1.1	0.1	0.5	0.3
Middlesbrough UA	36.1	3.6	0.7	0.1	0.4	0.1
Stockton-On-Tees UA	55.8	5.5	1.3	0.3	1.5	0.6
Cumbria	187.4	21.5	6.0	0.7	4.6	6.8
Durham	178.7	18.0	3.7	1.6	3.6	2.7
Northumberland	104.0	9.9	2.3	0.2	1.9	4.0
Tyne & Wear	278.6	26.3	4.3	1.5	5.3	0.9
Yorkshire & Humberside Region	1,611.3	171.8	47.7	6.8	41.5	24.8
Humberside	285.5	30.0	13.7	1.0	6.7	7.3
East Riding of Yorkshire UA	117.4	11.1	4.5	0.2	2.5	5.3
Kingston Upon Hull UA	62.7	7.1	3.6	0.5	1.7	0.2
North Lincolnshire UA	56.3	6.5	3.4	0.1	1.6	1.6
North East Lincolnshire UA	49.1	5.3	2.3	0.1	1.0	0.3
North Yorkshire	285.8	34.0	11.1	0.8	7.8	12.1
York UA	60.5	7.9	3.9	0.2	1.0	0.6
Rest of North Yorkshire	225.3	26.1	7.2	0.6	6.8	11.5
South Yorkshire	381.0	42.5	9.0	2.4	9.7	2.5
West Yorkshire	658.9	65.3	14.0	2.6	17.3	2.9
East Midland Region	1,534.0	164.2	49.8	5.6	34.9	29.5
Derbyshire	360.9	43.7	11.9	1.6	7.5	5.7
Leicestershire	347.0	34.1	10.2	1.2	6.5	4.1
Lincolnshire	243.5	27.9	9.7	1.0	5.6	13.3
Northamptonshire	243.9	23.9	7.4	0.8	7.8	2.8
Nottinghamshire	338.7	34.6	10.6	1.0	7.4	3.5
East Anglia Region	868.0	101.6	37.3	2.5	20.3	23.2
Cambridgeshire	277.0	34.1	10.6	0.8	6.5	6.9
Norfolk	321.9	38.1	14.5	1.0	6.2	9.8
Suffolk	269.2	29.4	12.3	0.6	7.6	6.5
South Eastern Region	6,996.2	685.3	207.9	20.0	100.1	36.8
Bedfordshire	214.9	21.8	5.6	0.8	3.6	2.2
Berkshire	383.8	36.0	9.1	0.9	6.2	1.6
Buckinghamshire	323.2	27.2	7.4	0.6	7.9	2.2
East Sussex	265.2	27.0	7.8	1.3	2.5	1.7
Essex	640.0	68.6	19.5	2.0	10.4	6.1
Greater London	2,286.5	220.5	66.4	8.3	31.1	1.9
Hampshire	669.8	62.7	24.1	1.2	7.9	6.3
Hertfordshire	493.0	50.1	12.8	0.7	7.5	2.5
Isle of Wight UA	47.7	5.8	2.5	0.2	0.4	0.5
Kent	597.0	59.6	20.1	1.8	8.9	4.8
Oxfordshire	240.8	23.8	9.2	0.7	3.7	3.3
Surrey	507.2	49.7	14.4	1.1	6.8	1.6
West Sussex	327.1	32.5	9.1	0.4	3.1	2.2
South Western Region	2,026.2	225.1	78.4	6.8	33.3	33.9
Avon	378.5	38.9	14.2	1.4	7.1	2.4
Bristol UA	137.4	15.7	5.0	1.0	2.9	0.2
North Somerset UA	76.6	6.8	2.6	0.2	1.4	0.6
Bath & North East Somerset UA	63.7	6.0	2.4	0.1	0.8	0.5
South Gloucestershire UA	100.9	10.3	4.2	0.1	2.1	1.1
Cornwall	185.7	23.9	8.6	0.8	2.6	5.4
Devonshire	399.7	50.1	17.0	1.8	5.3	9.6
Dorset	288.5	30.2	11.1	1.0	2.8	3.5
Gloucestershire	232.3	23.9	9.3	0.7	2.9	3.1
Somerset	202.1	25.9	8.0	0.6	6.8	5.6
Wiltshire	339.6	32.2	10.1	0.6	5.8	4.3

Table 8 (continued)

Thousands

Country/region/local authority	Special vehicles group	Other vehicles	Crown & other exempt vehicles	All vehicles	of which: body type cars	
					All	Per cent company
Great Britain	47.7	39.6	1,423.5	26,301.9	22,237.5	10.3
Vehicle Under Disposal	0.7	0.6	24.9	469.1	388.9	
County Uncoded	0.6	0.3	19.0	125.4	89.9	12.0
England	37.8	35.0	1,140.9	22,476.8	19,017.9	10.8
Northern Region	2.9	1.9	89.8	1,149.8	980.2	6.9
Cleveland	0.6	0.4	15.0	196.7	171.2	4.0
Hartlepool UA	0.1	0.1	2.6	28.4	24.9	3.4
Redcar & Cleveland UA	0.1	0.1	3.9	53.2	47.2	2.6
Middlesbrough UA	0.1	0.1	4.0	45.2	39.5	5.1
Stockton-On-Tees UA	0.5	0.1	4.4	69.9	59.5	4.6
Cumbria	0.9	0.5	16.1	244.5	197.5	9.7
Durham	0.4	0.4	21.6	230.8	197.1	4.2
Northumberland	0.3	0.2	8.4	131.2	110.4	4.1
Tyne & Wear	0.6	0.5	28.6	346.5	304.1	9.3
Yorkshire & Humberside Region	4.4	4.5	123.5	2,036.3	1,707.4	8.7
Humberside	1.0	1.0	20.1	366.4	300.0	6.6
East Riding of Yorkshire UA	0.3	0.3	7.6	149.1	122.2	5.0
Kingston Upon Hull UA	0.2	0.4	6.1	82.5	67.7	11.1
North Lincolnshire UA	0.4	0.2	3.9	74.0	59.0	5.9
North East Lincolnshire UA	0.1	0.1	2.5	60.8	51.1	5.4
North Yorkshire	1.2	0.7	17.7	371.2	296.1	7.5
York UA	0.2	0.2	2.8	77.2	62.3	8.4
Rest of North Yorkshire	1.0	0.5	14.9	294.0	233.7	7.2
South Yorkshire	0.9	1.1	39.0	488.0	414.5	7.0
West Yorkshire	1.4	1.7	46.8	810.7	696.9	11.1
East Midland Region	4.6	3.9	106.2	1,932.6	1,609.0	9.3
Derbyshire	1.2	1.0	26.0	459.4	379.7	10.4
Leicestershire	0.8	0.8	20.1	424.8	360.8	11.2
Lincolnshire	1.0	0.8	19.2	322.1	255.3	6.2
Northamptonshire	0.7	0.5	14.3	302.1	253.3	10.7
Nottinghamshire	1.0	0.8	26.6	424.2	359.9	7.6
East Anglia Region	3.1	2.2	54.3	1,112.5	901.8	7.4
Cambridgeshire	0.7	0.6	15.5	352.7	286.7	7.8
Norfolk	1.5	0.8	21.1	415.0	334.6	8.4
Suffolk	0.9	0.7	17.6	344.8	280.4	5.8
South Eastern Region	9.0	9.9	325.6	8,390.8	7,223.3	11.1
Bedfordshire	0.5	0.3	10.8	260.6	222.0	10.1
Berkshire	0.5	0.4	12.3	450.7	392.0	20.7
Buckinghamshire	0.3	0.3	12.8	382.0	331.9	15.8
East Sussex	0.2	0.5	15.5	321.8	276.3	4.7
Essex	1.2	1.2	35.8	784.8	665.4	5.4
Greater London	1.9	2.3	100.9	2,719.9	2,361.8	13.8
Hampshire	1.1	1.1	33.9	808.1	692.4	7.1
Hertfordshire	0.7	0.6	17.9	585.6	505.3	17.6
Isle of Wight UA	0.1	0.1	3.8	61.0	50.2	2.7
Kent	1.0	1.4	34.3	728.9	619.8	5.6
Oxfordshire	0.5	0.4	11.8	294.2	248.1	8.5
Surrey	0.6	0.6	20.6	602.6	521.0	9.2
West Sussex	0.5	0.5	15.2	390.6	337.3	8.6
South Western Region	4.3	4.5	127.9	2,540.4	2,109.3	9.9
Avon	0.6	0.8	20.3	464.2	392.6	8.5
Bristol UA	0.2	0.3	7.4	170.2	142.9	14.6
North Somerset UA	0.1	0.2	4.5	92.8	79.6	5.6
Bath & North East Somerset UA	0.1	0.1	3.0	76.7	65.6	5.1
South Gloucestershire UA	0.2	0.2	5.4	124.5	104.5	4.4
Cornwall	0.6	0.7	16.8	245.1	196.6	3.8
Devonshire	1.0	1.0	29.1	514.6	419.2	4.5
Dorset	0.5	0.6	18.0	356.2	300.4	4.4
Gloucestershire	0.5	0.4	14.5	287.6	241.3	6.2
Somerset	0.6	0.5	14.3	264.5	210.5	5.0
Wiltshire	0.5	0.5	14.7	408.2	348.7	31.5

Table 8 (continued)

Thousands

Private and light goods

Country/region/local authority	Body type cars	Other vehicles	Motor cycles scooters and mopeds	Public transport vehicles	Goods	Special concession
West Midland Region	2,082.3	266.6	51.5	6.8	50.8	20.9
Hereford & Worcestershire	307.6	35.0	10.1	0.9	5.5	6.0
Salop	172.3	21.7	5.1	0.4	4.0	5.5
Staffordshire	389.5	39.7	12.6	1.9	10.6	4.4
Warwickshire	250.4	26.3	7.0	0.6	4.0	2.8
West Midlands	962.5	143.9	16.8	3.1	26.7	2.2
North Western Region	2,149.6	230.1	48.5	8.7	54.9	12.5
Cheshire	388.8	38.3	11.7	0.9	8.9	4.2
Greater Manchester	905.4	107.7	14.9	3.5	27.3	2.2
Lancashire	476.9	49.6	13.9	1.9	11.7	5.2
Merseyside	378.6	34.6	8.1	2.4	6.9	1.0
Scotland	1,572.6	160.9	25.2	8.7	32.1	32.1
Aberdeen City UA	73.6	7.0	1.4	0.6	1.6	0.4
Aberdeenshire UA	88.0	10.1	1.9	0.3	2.3	5.2
Angus UA	38.9	4.0	0.8	0.1	0.7	2.0
Argyll & Bute UA	30.3	3.9	0.6	0.1	0.6	0.8
The Scottish Borders UA	39.4	5.2	0.7	0.1	0.8	2.4
Clackmannanshire UA	15.0	1.2	0.3	-	0.2	0.2
West Dunbartonshire UA	23.2	1.7	0.2	-	0.2	0.1
Dumfries & Galloway UA	52.8	6.7	1.4	0.1	1.7	3.8
City of Dundee UA	38.2	3.2	0.5	0.3	1.1	0.3
East Ayrshire UA	34.0	3.3	0.5	0.1	0.7	1.0
East Dunbartonshire UA	39.1	2.5	0.4	-	0.5	0.1
East Lothian UA	28.9	2.7	0.6	-	0.4	0.9
East Renfrewshire UA	31.2	1.5	0.3	0.1	0.3	0.1
City of Endinburgh UA	154.1	14.4	2.1	0.8	2.1	0.5
Falkirk UA	44.9	3.6	0.7	0.5	1.0	0.5
Fife UA	112.0	9.6	2.0	0.5	1.5	1.9
City of Glasgow UA	124.6	18.2	1.1	1.4	3.6	0.4
Highland UA	70.9	10.4	1.9	0.4	1.5	2.4
Inverclyde UA	22.3	1.3	0.3	0.2	0.2	0.1
Midlothian UA	26.1	2.6	0.5	0.3	0.3	0.3
Moray UA	30.9	3.4	0.9	0.1	0.6	1.3
North Ayrshire UA	38.2	3.2	0.7	0.2	0.6	0.5
North Lanarkshire UA	80.2	7.5	0.6	0.4	2.4	0.3
Orkney Islands UA	7.1	1.4	0.3	0.1	0.2	0.8
Perth & Kinross UA	50.9	5.6	0.8	0.1	0.8	2.4
Renfrewshire UA	49.0	3.5	0.5	0.4	1.0	0.3
Shetland Islands UA	8.0	2.0	0.3	0.1	0.2	0.2
South Ayrshire UA	38.8	3.1	0.6	0.5	0.7	0.7
South Lanarkshire UA	87.4	7.2	0.9	0.4	1.6	1.0
Stirling UA	39.6	4.5	0.4	0.1	0.9	0.6
West Lothian UA	46.9	4.5	0.8	0.2	1.3	0.5
Western Isles UA	8.2	1.6	0.1	0.1	0.3	0.2
Wales	974.3	111.6	22.4	5.0	18.0	16.6
Aberconwy & Colwyn UA	40.0	5.4	1.0	0.4	0.5	0.8
Anglesey UA	26.4	3.4	0.8	0.1	0.4	0.7
Blaenau Gwent UA	18.3	1.5	0.5	0.1	0.3	-
Bridgend UA	41.4	3.7	1.0	0.2	0.7	0.2
Caernarfonshire & Merionethshire UA	40.8	6.8	1.0	0.2	0.7	1.4
Caerphilly UA	48.3	4.6	1.0	0.2	0.8	0.2
Cardiff UA	111.9	8.7	1.4	0.4	1.8	0.2
Cardiganshire UA	24.9	4.5	0.6	0.2	0.5	1.3
Carmarthenshire UA	59.0	8.2	1.4	0.3	1.6	1.8
Denbighshire UA	33.8	4.3	0.8	0.1	0.6	0.8
Flintshire UA	57.6	6.3	1.6	0.2	1.5	0.6
Merthyr Tydfil UA	14.1	1.4	0.2	-	0.2	-
Monmouthshire UA	34.0	3.8	1.0	0.1	0.6	0.9
Neath & Port Talbot UA	39.2	3.8	1.2	0.3	0.5	0.2
Newport UA	42.1	6.0	0.9	0.1	1.4	0.3
Pembrokeshire UA	41.3	6.2	1.1	0.2	0.8	1.9
Powys UA	48.2	9.5	1.2	0.3	1.6	3.5
Rhondda, Cynon, Taff UA	65.6	6.1	1.3	0.5	1.1	0.2
Swansea UA	73.3	6.9	1.3	0.5	0.9	0.3
Torfaen UA	29.4	3.0	0.8	0.4	0.3	0.1
The Vale of Glamorgan UA	43.2	3.4	1.0	0.1	0.5	0.4
Wrexham UA	41.3	4.0	1.2	0.1	0.7	0.7

Table 8 (continued)

Country/region/local authority	Special vehicles group	Other vehicles	Crown & other exempt vehicles	All vehicles	of which: body type cars All	Per cent company
West Midland Region	5.5	4.4	132.8	2,621.6	2,183.1	16.0
Hereford & Worcestershire	0.6	0.6	20.0	386.2	320.3	10.5
Salop	0.6	0.4	12.5	222.5	180.8	8.4
Staffordshire	0.9	1.0	29.6	490.2	412.6	6.8
Warwickshire	1.4	0.5	13.6	306.5	259.9	23.0
West Midlands	2.0	1.9	57.1	1,216.3	1,009.5	21.0
North Western Region	4.0	3.9	180.8	2,692.9	2,303.8	11.6
Cheshire	0.8	0.7	27.6	481.7	410.8	6.9
Greater Manchester	1.9	1.5	62.1	1,126.6	958.8	19.4
Lancashire	0.9	1.1	39.1	600.2	508.6	5.6
Merseyside	0.3	0.6	51.9	484.4	425.6	5.5
Scotland	6.4	1.9	126.4	1,966.4	1,674.2	8.7
Aberdeen City UA	0.4	0.1	3.1	88.4	75.9	10.0
Aberdeenshire UA	0.9	0.1	4.8	113.6	90.6	5.2
Angus UA	0.2	0.1	2.3	49.0	40.4	5.2
Argyll & Bute UA	0.2	-	1.8	38.4	31.5	3.7
The Scottish Borders UA	0.2	0.1	2.2	51.0	40.8	7.1
Clackmannanshire UA	-	-	1.4	18.5	16.4	3.0
West Dunbartonshire UA	-	-	2.3	27.9	25.4	3.7
Dumfries & Galloway UA	0.3	0.1	4.2	71.1	55.5	5.4
City of Dundee UA	0.2	0.1	3.5	47.4	41.0	6.7
East Ayrshire UA	0.2	-	3.6	43.4	37.2	4.5
East Dunbartonshire UA	0.1	-	2.0	44.7	40.9	3.2
East Lothian UA	0.1	-	2.0	35.8	30.5	3.8
East Renfrewshire UA	0.1	-	1.5	35.1	32.5	2.5
City of Endinburgh UA	0.2	0.1	10.9	185.2	160.4	23.9
Falkirk UA	0.2	0.1	3.3	54.8	47.7	4.0
Fife UA	0.3	0.1	8.8	136.8	119.5	4.1
City of Glasgow UA	0.4	0.1	16.8	166.7	140.2	18.6
Highland UA	0.6	0.1	5.1	93.3	74.0	5.0
Inverclyde UA	-	-	2.1	26.5	24.3	3.6
Midlothian UA	-	-	2.2	32.3	28.0	6.6
Moray UA	0.3	0.1	1.6	39.1	31.9	4.6
North Ayrshire UA	0.1	-	4.3	47.7	42.1	3.5
North Lanarkshire UA	0.3	0.1	11.1	102.8	90.7	4.2
Orkney Islands UA	0.1	-	0.8	10.9	7.4	5.1
Perth & Kinross UA	0.2	0.1	2.6	63.5	52.5	7.9
Renfrewshire UA	0.1	-	4.3	59.3	52.9	5.7
Shetland Islands UA	0.1	-	0.5	11.5	8.2	5.6
South Ayrshire UA	0.2	0.1	2.7	47.4	41.1	7.1
South Lanarkshire UA	0.2	0.1	8.6	107.4	94.9	5.0
Stirling UA	0.1	-	2.1	48.3	41.3	30.6
West Lothian UA	0.1	0.1	3.4	57.7	50.0	4.5
Western Isles UA	0.1	-	0.5	11.1	8.4	3.7
Wales	2.2	1.8	112.3	1,264.2	1,066.7	6.3
Aberconwy & Colwyn UA	0.1	0.1	3.8	52.2	43.0	3.9
Anglesey UA	0.1	-	2.6	34.6	28.4	2.3
Blaenau Gwent UA	-	-	3.4	24.1	21.5	2.7
Bridgend UA	0.1	0.1	5.9	53.3	47.0	5.2
Caernarfonshire & Merionethshire UA	0.2	0.1	4.2	55.4	43.6	3.4
Caerphilly UA	0.1	0.1	8.0	63.3	55.9	2.9
Cardiff UA	0.1	0.1	6.9	131.5	117.8	23.3
Cardiganshire UA	0.1	0.1	2.7	34.9	26.4	3.2
Carmarthenshire UA	0.2	0.1	8.7	81.3	65.4	2.9
Denbighshire UA	0.1	0.1	3.6	44.2	36.4	4.9
Flintshire UA	0.1	0.1	4.9	72.8	61.5	5.9
Merthyr Tydfil UA	-	-	3.4	19.5	17.4	2.6
Monmouthshire UA	0.1	0.1	2.4	43.0	35.6	3.7
Neath & Port Talbot UA	0.1	0.1	7.1	52.5	45.8	2.9
Newport UA	0.1	0.1	3.6	54.7	45.2	6.8
Pembrokeshire UA	0.2	0.1	4.7	56.4	44.3	3.3
Powys UA	0.2	0.1	5.0	69.6	50.8	4.8
Rhondda, Cynon, Taff UA	0.1	0.1	10.0	85.0	74.9	3.1
Swansea UA	-	0.1	8.1	91.5	80.4	6.0
Torfaen UA	-	-	4.8	38.8	33.5	7.3
The Vale of Glamorgan UA	-	-	3.5	52.4	46.1	3.8
Wrexham UA	0.1	0.1	4.9	53.2	45.5	3.9

Table 9 Motor vehicles currently licensed:[1] Historic series: 1903-1985

For detail of years 1986-1996 see table 1

Thousands

| Year | Private and light goods [2] | | Goods vehicles [3,4] | Motorcylces scooters and mopeds [5] | Public transport vehicles [6] | Special machines etc [7] | Other vehicles [8] | Crown and exempt vehicles [9] | All vehicles |
	Private cars	Other vehicles							
1903	8		4	..	5	..	..	..	17
1909	53		30	36	24	..	..	..	143
1920	187		101	228	75	..	..	..	591
1930	1,056		349	712	101	15	15	24	2,272
1939	2,034		488	418	90	31	3	84	3,148
1946	1,770		560	449	105	146	16	61	3,107
1950	1,979	439	439	643	123	262	24	61	3,970
1951	2,095	457	451	725	123	250	26	63	4,190
1952	2,221	477	450	812	119	270	29	86	4,464
1953	2,446	516	446	889	105	289	30	88	4,809
1954	2,733	566	450	977	97	307	32	88	5,250
1955	3,109	633	462	1,076	92	326	35	89	5,822
1956	3,437	685	471	1,137	89	336	37	95	6,287
1957	3,707	723	473	1,261	87	355	41	96	6,743
1958	4,047	772	461	1,300	86	367	46	96	7,175
1959	4,416	824	473	1,479	83	383	55	96	7,809
1960	4,900	894	493	1,583	84	392	65	101	8,512
1961	5,296	944	508	1,577	82	400	76	106	8,989
1962	5,776	1,002	512	1,567	84	401	83	107	9,532
1963	6,462	1,092	535	1,546	86	412	88	115	10,336
1964	7,190	1,184	551	1,534	86	421	90	120	11,176
1965	7,732	1,240	584	1,420	86	417	91	127	11,697
1966	8,210	1,283	577	1,239	85	399	87	142	12,022
1967	8,882	1,358	593	1,190	85	416	89	147	12,760
1968	9,285	1,388	580	1,082	89	409	92	157	13,082
1969	9,672	1,408	547	993	92	398	90	162	13,362
1970	9,971	1,421	545	923	93	385	89	121	13,548
1971	10,443	1,452	542	899	96	380	92	126	14,030
1972	11,006	1,498	525	866	95	371	95	128	14,584
1973	11,738	1,559	540	887	96	373	97	137	15,427
1974	11,917	1,547	539	918	96	380	96	149	15,642
1975	12,526	1,592	553	1,077	105	384	108	166	16,511
1976	13,184	1,626	563	1,175	110	387	117	156	17,318
1977	13,220	1,591	559	1,190	110	393	115	167	17,345
1978	13,626	1,597	549	1,194	110	394	111	177	17,758
1979	14,162	1,623	561	1,292	111	402	106	359	18,616
1980	14,660	1,641	507	1,372	110	397	100	412	19,199
1981	14,867	1,623	489	1,371	110	365	95	427	19,347
1982	15,264	1,624	477	1,370	111	371	91	454	19,762
1983	15,543	1,692	488	1,290	113	376	86	621	20,209
1984	16,055	1,752	490	1,225	116	375	82	670	20,765
1985	16,454	1,805	485	1,148	120	374	78	695	21,159

1 The annual vehicle census of licensed vehicles has been taken as follows: 1903-1910 at 31 December; 1911-1920 at 31 March; 1921-1925 for the highest quarter; 1926-1938 for the September quarter; 1939-1945 at 31 August; 1946-1976 for the September quarter; 1977 census results are estimates; 1978 onward at 31 December.
2 From 1950 onwards, retrospective counts within the October 1982 taxation classes have been estimated. For years up to 1990, retrospective counts within these new taxation classes have been estimated. See Notes on taxation class changes.
3 Includes agricultural vans and lorries, showmens' goods vehicles licensed to draw trailers (note 2 applies).
4 Excludes electric goods vehicles which are now exempt from licence duty.
5 Includes scooters and mopeds.
6 Includes taxis. Prior to 1969, tram cars were included.
7 Includes agricultural tractors, combine harvesters, mowing machines, digging machines, mobile cranes and works trucks.
8 Includes three-wheelers, showmens' haulage and recovery vehicles.
9 Includes electric vehicles which during this period were exempt from licence duty and personal and direct export vehicles.

Table 10 Motor vehicles registered for the first time: by taxation group[1]: 1986-96

Thousands

| | Private and light goods [2] | | Public transportation vehicles | | | | | |
| | Body type cars | Other vehicles | Motor cycles scooters and mopeds | Hackney taxation class [3] | *Of which:* Bus taxation class [4] | Goods [6] | Special machines/ special concession [7] | All other vehicles [9] |
Year								
1986	1,839.3	231.4	106.4	8.9	5.5 [5]	51.4	34.8	61.5
1987	1,962.7	249.9	90.8	8.7	5.0 [5]	54.0	37.7	70.1
1988	2,154.7	282.3	90.1	9.2	5.0 [5]	63.4	45.2	78.6
1989	2,241.2	294.0	97.3	8.0	5.1 [5]	64.5	42.5	81.4
1990	1,942.3	237.6	94.4	7.4	4.5 [5]	44.4	34.2	78.4
1991	1,536.6	171.9	76.5	5.2	3.0 [5]	28.6	26.1	76.6
1992	1,528.0	166.4	65.6	5.1	3.1 [5]	28.7	24.1	83.9
1993	1,694.6	158.8	58.4	5.4	3.6 [5]	32.8	30.0	89.0
1994	1,809.1	182.6	64.6	6.7	4.2 [5]	41.1	35.3	104.7
1995	1,828.3	195.7	68.9	..	5.2	48.0	33.3 [8]	127.1
1996	1,888.4	205.0	89.6	..	6.5	45.5	25.7	149.5

continued

| | | | body type cars in all taxation classes | | | | | |
| | | | | *of which:* | | | | |
Year	All vehicles	All body type cars	Company	Imported	Diesel	Per cent company	Per cent imports	Per cent diesel
1986	2,333.7	1,883.2	867.7	1,018.0	74.9	*46*	*54*	*4*
1987	2,473.9	2,016.2	969.8	1,015.6	89.9	*48*	*50*	*4*
1988	2,723.5	2,210.3	1,131.4	1,216.0	99.2	*51*	*55*	*4*
1989	2,828.9	2,304.4	1,175.5	1,272.3	123.2	*51*	*55*	*5*
1990	2,438.7	2,005.1	1,049.9	1,117.5	125.4	*52*	*56*	*6*
1991	1,921.5	1,600.1	833.1	874.2	137.4	*52*	*55*	*9*
1992	1,901.8	1,599.1	826.7	874.5	195.8	*52*	*55*	*12*
1993	2,074.0	1,776.5	910.1	991.5	327.8	*51*	*56*	*18*
1994	2,249.0	1,906.4	996.4	1,082.1	418.8	*52*	*57*	*22*
1995	2,306.5	1,938.1	1,022.4	1,132.3	395.9	*53*	*58*	*20*
1996	2,410.1	2,018.3	1,056.7	1,246.1	358.4	*52*	*62*	*18*

1 See notes and definitions.
2 For years up to 1990 retrospective counts within these new taxation classes have been estimated.
3 Taxation class 35, Hackney. Public transportation vehicles including taxis: Abolished 30th June 1995
4 Taxation class 34, Buses. Public transportation vehicles with more than 8 seats. Introduced 1st July 1995.
5 Estimated: Retrospective estimates are based on vehicles registrations in tax class 35, with more than 8 seats
6 Until 30th June 1995 included agricultural vans and lorries and showman's goods vehicles licensed to draw trailers.
   From 1st July 1995 separate taxation groups for farmers and showmen were abolished.
7 The agricultural and special machines taxation group was abolished on 30th June 1995 and replaced by the
   special concession taxation group from 1st July 1995.
8 The figure shown is aggregate number of vehicles registered in 1995 between 1st January and 30th June in agricultural
   and special machines group, and between 1st July and 31st December in special concession group.
9 Includes crown and exempt vehicles, three wheelers, and others.

Table 11 Motor vehicles registered for the first time: by taxation group, vehicle details: 1986 - 1996

(a) Private and light goods: by engine size
Thousands

Over	Not over	1986	1987	1988	1989	1990	1991	1992	1993	1994	1995	1996
	1,000 cc	236.3	245.5	260.5	222.0	162.0	104.3	64.7	73.4	78.6	76.5	67.8
1,000 cc	1,200 cc	205.9	198.2	195.8	196.2	183.0	153.4	176.3	180.8	184.1	203.8	188.7
1,200 cc	1,500 cc	508.1	520.7	576.6	600.5	531.0	406.2	412.3	415.5	415.2	387.4	427.8
1,500 cc	1,800 cc	689.8	723.4	782.5	799.6	681.0	557.2	521.7	576.2	623.7	650.3	642.0
1,800 cc	2,000 cc	234.1	312.7	387.5	462.2	403.0	321.6	344.4	405.3	427.2	399.3	450.8
2,000 cc	2,500 cc	104.7	111.8	108.5	109.7	102.0	104.4	115.1	135.1	184.6	206.8	207.4
2,500 cc	3,000 cc	43.3	45.8	57.4	66.5	56.0	38.2	34.5	33.8	43.6	60.5	63.1
3,000 cc		24.6	26.2	34.6	37.2	32.7	23.2	25.3	33.3	34.5	39.4	45.5
cc not known		0.3	0.1	0.1	0.1	0.1	0.1	0.1	0.1	0.1	0.0	0.1
All vehicles		2,047.2	2,184.3	2,403.6	2,494.0	2151.7	1,708.5	1,694.2	1,853.4	1,991.6	2,024.0	2093.3

Of which: Private and light goods: Diesel propulsion
Thousands

Over	Not over	1986	1987	1988	1989	1990	1991	1992	1993	1994	1995	1996
	1,000 cc									0.6	0.8	0.6
1,000 cc	1,200 cc									0.4	0.3	0.3
1,200 cc	1,500 cc									29.4	9.4	3.9
1,500 cc	1,800 cc									210.9	217.8	169.5
1,800 cc	2,000 cc									174.9	157.4	177.0
2,000 cc	2,500 cc									130.0	149.3	146.5
2,500 cc	3,000 cc									15.7	20.7	24.6
3,000 cc										6.0	5.5	4.8
cc not known										-	-	-
All vehicles										568.0	561.3	527.3

(b) Motor cycles, scooters and mopeds: by engine size
Thousands

Over	Not over	1986	1987	1988	1989	1990	1991	1992	1993	1994	1995	1996
	50 cc	37.5	29.7	24.7	22.9	18.8	13.1	9.1	6.5	6.9	6.3	8.9
50 cc	150 cc	41.8	34.0	31.9	32.4	29.1	18.8	14.7	11.2	10.5	10.2	13.0
150 cc	200 cc	1.1	0.9	1.5	1.7	1.5	1.1	0.7	0.6	0.7	0.6	0.6
200 cc	250 cc	3.3	3.6	4.1	5.6	6.0	4.6	4.2	3.6	3.6	3.7	4.1
250 cc	350 cc	3.3	2.7	2.8	2.7	2.5	2.2	2.0	1.9	1.7	1.4	1.1
350 cc	500 cc	3.8	3.3	3.2	3.5	4.2	5.2	5.3	4.9	6.8	7.6	11.3
500 cc		15.7	16.6	21.8	28.6	32.2	31.5	29.5	29.9	34.3	38.7	50.4
All vehicles		106.4	90.8	90.1	97.3	94.4	76.5	65.6	58.4	64.6	68.9	89.6

(c) Public transport vehicles: by seating capacity
Thousands

Over	Not over	1986	1987	1988	1989	1990	1991	1992	1993	1994	1995	1996
	4 seats	2.9	2.2	1.2	0.6	0.2	0.1	0.1	0.1	0.5	0.0	
4 seats	8 seats	0.5	1.4	3.0	2.4	2.7	2.1	2.0	1.7	2.1	1.3	
8 seats or less		3.4	3.6	4.2	3.0	2.9	2.2	2.0	1.8	2.5	1.3	
8 seats	32 seats	3.5	3.6	2.7	2.3	2.2	1.6	1.4	1.7	1.9	2.1	3.1
32 seats	48 seats	0.2	0.2	0.2	0.3	0.5	0.3	0.6	0.8	1.2	1.4	1.4
48 seats		1.8	1.3	2.0	2.5	1.8	1.1	1.0	1.2	1.0	1.7	2.0
All over 8 seats		5.5	5.0	5.0	5.1	4.5	3.0	3.1	3.6	4.2	5.2	6.5
All capacities		8.9	8.7	9.2	8.2	7.7	5.2	5.1	5.4	6.7		

Table 11 (continued)

(d) Goods: by gross weight
Thousands

Over	Not over	1988	1989	1990	1991	1992	1993	1994	1995	1996
	3.5 tonnes	1.2	1.0	0.7	0.6	0.5	0.5	0.5	0.3	0.0
3.5 tonnes	7.5 tonnes	21.5	21.6	17.0	10.8	10.4	10.4	12.6	14.1	14.1
7.5 tonnes	12 tonnes	1.9	2.0	1.6	1.1	1.2	1.3	1.0	1.2	1.3
12 tonnes	25 tonnes	18.6	18.8	13.1	8.0	7.6	8.7	10.5	12.6	12.3
25 tonnes	33 tonnes	8.9	8.9	4.8	3.1	3.2	3.9	5.9	5.9	4.7
33 tonnes	38 tonnes	11.3	12.2	7.2	5.0	5.9	8.1	10.5	13.5	12.6
38 tonnes	40 tonnes	0.0	0.0	0.0	0.0	0.0	0.0	0.0	0.0	0.0
40 tonnes								0.1	0.5	0.4
Gross weight unknown		-	-	-	-	-	-	-	-	-
All vehicles		63.4	64.5	44.4	28.6	28.7	32.8	41.1	48.0	45.5

(e) Special machines, agricultural tractors etc.
Thousands

	1986	1987	1988	1989	1990	1991	1992	1993	1994	1995	1996
Agricultural tractors	18.6	19.6	21.8	19.3	17.6	14.6	13.9	17.7	18.3	19.0	18.7
Combine harvesters and other agricultural	2.6	2.7	3.0	3.0	2.8	2.4	2.5	2.5	2.5	3.3	3.7
Mowing machines	1.8	1.8	1.8	2.0	1.7	1.1	1.2	1.0	1.1	0.9	0.9
Electric										0.2	0.4
Gritting vehicle										0.1	0.1
Others	2.2	2.2	2.3	2.4	2.2	1.7	1.8	2.6	3.2	3.8	1.8
All vehicles	34.8	37.7	45.2	42.6	34.2	26.1	24.1	30.0	35.3	33.3	25.7

(f) Other licenced vehicles
Thousands

	1986	1987	1988	1989	1990	1991	1992	1993	1994	1995	1996
Tricycles	2.6	2.2	2.1	1.5	1.2	0.3	1.2	1.0	0.9	0.6	0.7
General haulage	0.4	0.4	0.4	0.2	0.1	0.1	0.1	0.1	..	0.0	0.0
Recovery vehicles	.	.	0.9	0.9	0.7	0.4	0.3	0.3	0.3	0.3	0.3
All vehicles	3.0	2.6	3.4	2.6	2.1	0.7	1.6	1.4	1.3	1.0	1.0

(g) Crown and other vehicles exempt from licence duty
Thousands

	1986	1987	1988	1989	1990	1991	1992	1993	1994	1995	1996
Crown vehicles	5.3	4.6	4.1	4.4	4.0	3.2	3.7	3.1	4.1	3.3	1.2
Personal and direct export vehicles	9.3	10.8	9.9	9.9	9.1	8.9	7.1	7.5	9.3	9.3	11.8
Other exempt vehicles	44.0	52.2	56.1	64.4	63.1	63.8	71.6	81.9	95.0	108.8	127.3
All exempt vehicles	58.5	67.5	70.1	78.6	76.2	75.8	82.3	92.4	108.4	121.4	140.3

(i) Special vehicles group: Tax classes 14 and 15

	1986	1987	1988	1989	1990	1991	1992	1993	1994	1995	1996
Special vehicles										3.3	8.1

(j) Other abolished tax groups (In 1995, covers Jan - Jun only)
Thousands

	1986	1987	1988	1989	1990	1991	1992	1993	1994	1995	1996
Digging machines	5.1	6.1	8.5	7.5	5.5	3.7	2.9	3.9	5.8	3.2	
Mobile cranes	0.5	0.4	0.9	0.9	0.8	0.3	0.2	0.2	0.3	0.2	
Works trucks	4.0	4.9	7.0	7.4	3.7	2.3	1.7	2.1	4.1	2.5	

Table 12 Motor vehicles registered for the first time: by county: 1996 with related stock and ownership information.

Country/region/county	1986 All vehicles currently licensed (thousands)	1996 All vehicles New registrations (thousands)	1996 All vehicles Currently licensed (thousands)	1996 Car in all taxation classes New registrations (thousands)	1996 Car in all taxation classes Currently licensed (thousands)	Per 1,000 population [1]	Average vehicle age (years) [2]
Great Britain	21,699	2,417.0	26,301.9	2,020.7	22,237.5	390	7.3
Vehicle under disposal	-	n/a	469.1	n/a	388.9	n/a	8.7
County uncoded	12	40.8	125.4	32.6	89.9	n/a	8.4
England	19,073	2,107.5	22,476.8	1,761.6	19,017.9	389	7.4
Northern Region	956	106.1	1,149.8	90.0	980.2	317	6.8
Cleveland	184	17.0	196.7	14.2	171.2	306	7.1
Cumbria	200	19.6	244.5	16.1	197.5	403	7.2
Durham	182	18.0	230.8	15.0	197.1	324	6.7
Northumberland	95	9.6	131.2	8.1	110.4	359	6.5
Tyne and Wear	295	41.9	346.5	36.6	304.1	269	6.5
Yorkshire and Humberside Region	1,715	172.2	2,036.3	138.4	1,707.4	339	6.8
Humberside	312	27.8	366.4	22.3	300.0	337	7.1
North Yorkshire	298	29.1	371.2	22.0	296.1	405	6.7
South Yorkshire	423	41.0	488.0	32.0	414.5	318	7.2
West Yorkshire	682	74.4	810.7	62.2	696.9	331	6.5
East Midlands Region	1,539	171.1	1,932.6	140.4	1,609.0	390	7.4
Derbyshire	295	46.5	459.4	36.7	379.7	396	7.2
Leicestershire	350	52.6	424.8	46.7	360.8	391	7.4
Lincolnshire	270	19.2	322.1	14.3	255.3	417	7.5
Northamptonshire	236	21.9	302.1	17.6	253.3	423	7.2
Nottinghamshire	389	30.9	424.2	25.0	359.9	349	7.4
East Anglia Region	952	76.1	1,112.5	56.8	901.8	425	7.9
Cambridgeshire	299	28.0	352.7	20.7	286.7	413	7.6
Norfolk	357	26.8	415.0	20.6	334.6	433	7.9
Suffolk	296	21.2	344.8	15.5	280.4	427	8.1
South Eastern Region	7,494	828.5	8,390.8	712.0	7,223.3	402	7.6
Bedfordshire	245	20.2	260.6	17.0	222.0	407	7.4
Berkshire	381	61.0	450.7	53.9	392.0	500	6.6
Buckinghamshire	264	51.7	382.0	44.8	331.9	498	6.7
East Sussex	293	16.9	321.8	13.7	276.3	378	8.3
Essex	673	65.0	784.8	55.4	665.4	422	7.9
Greater London	2,628	316.1	2,719.9	276.7	2,361.8	337	7.7
Hampshire	687	56.0	808.1	45.9	692.4	428	7.9
Hertfordshire	521	80.8	585.6	70.6	505.3	500	6.8
Isle of Wight	55	2.7	61.0	2.2	50.2	401	9.3
Kent	659	46.4	728.9	37.6	619.8	400	8.0
Oxfordshire	259	28.1	294.2	24.0	248.1	415	7.5
Surrey	510	55.0	602.6	46.6	521.0	499	7.5
West Sussex	320	28.6	390.6	23.5	337.3	461	7.8

1 Using mid year 1995 population estimates.
2 Nominal: Vehicles registered at any time in 1996 are counted as age 1 year at the end of 1996,
   vehicles registered in 1995 are counted as age 2 at the end of 1995, etc, etc.

Table 12 (continued)

Country/region/county	1986 All vehicles currently licensed (thousands)	1996 All vehicles		1996 Car in all taxation classes			
		New registrations (thousands)	Currently licensed (thousands)	New registrations (thousands)	Currently licensed (thousands)	Per 1,000 population [1]	Average vehicle age (years) [2]
South Western Region	2,149	157.1	2,540.4	130.3	2,109.3	437	8.0
Avon	427	11.4	464.2	9.7	392.6	400	8.1
Cornwall	214	11.0	245.1	8.4	196.6	407	8.7
Devonshire	449	27.7	514.6	21.2	419.2	396	8.5
Dorset	313	18.5	356.2	14.8	300.4	443	8.6
Gloucestershire	255	16.6	287.6	13.6	241.3	437	8.1
Somerset	219	12.3	264.5	8.5	210.5	438	8.6
Wiltshire	273	59.6	408.2	54.0	348.7	590	6.3
West Midlands Region	2,076	329.8	2,621.6	274.8	2,183.1	411	6.9
Hereford & Worcs	303	35.5	386.2	30.7	320.3	461	7.6
Salop	178	15.5	222.5	11.5	180.8	431	7.5
Staffordshire	386	36.3	490.2	28.0	412.6	391	7.3
Warwickshire	189	32.6	306.5	27.6	259.9	521	6.5
West Midlands	1,020	209.9	1,216.3	176.9	1,009.5	383	6.5
North Western Region	2,195	266.6	2,692.9	219.0	2,303.8	359	6.8
Cheshire	382	40.1	481.7	32.7	410.8	420	6.9
Gtr Manchester	848	138.6	1,126.6	112.9	958.8	372	6.4
Lancashire	562	46.0	600.2	37.3	508.6	357	7.3
Merseyside	403	41.9	484.4	36.1	425.6	298	7.1
Wales	1,064	86.1	1,264.2	72.8	1,066.7	366	7.4
Scotland	1,562	182.6	1,966.4	153.8	1,674.2	326	6.3

1 Using mid year 1995 population estimates.
2 Nominal: Vehicles registered at any time in 1996 are counted as age 1 year at the end of 1996,
  vehicles registered in 1995 are counted as age 2 at the end of 1995, etc, etc.

Table 13 Monthly vehicle registrations: Seasonally adjusted series: 1992-1996[1]

Thousands

Year	Month	Cars	of which:		Motor cycles	Goods	All vehicles
			Imported cars	Company cars			
1992	January	129.4	68.5	69.5	6.1	2.3	154.7
	February	122.1	68.0	64.6	5.6	2.3	147.7
	March	123.9	68.9	63.4	5.4	2.5	149.1
	April	144.2	78.0	71.2	5.6	2.2	168.5
	May	130.0	72.9	68.2	5.8	2.1	156.6
	June	130.5	73.7	66.9	5.7	2.4	157.2
	July	128.0	70.9	66.4	5.8	2.7	151.7
	August	131.2	70.6	69.0	5.2	2.4	156.8
	September	130.6	70.8	66.9	4.6	2.3	153.8
	October	134.3	73.4	71.5	4.5	2.7	157.1
	November	133.3	72.5	69.3	4.5	2.5	157.4
	December	161.6	86.4	79.7	6.6	2.4	191.1
	All 1992	1599.1	874.5	826.7	65.6	28.7	1901.8
1993	January	136.2	76.1	67.6	5.4	2.2	161.9
	February	141.7	76.9	73.4	6.0	2.5	166.6
	March	140.0	76.8	74.1	5.6	2.1	164.2
	April	143.9	78.3	75.6	5.4	2.4	168.0
	May	146.6	81.0	77.6	5.4	2.5	172.0
	June	143.6	78.9	74.2	4.9	2.7	167.9
	July	147.0	83.3	72.6	4.7	2.5	168.6
	August	154.3	86.8	79.0	4.5	2.9	179.5
	September	150.6	86.5	77.6	4.0	4.2	176.4
	October	158.4	87.7	79.0	3.7	2.5	182.7
	November	161.7	91.6	81.3	4.3	3.2	188.1
	December	152.4	87.6	78.9	4.5	3.0	178.2
	All 1993	1776.5	991.5	910.1	58.4	32.8	2074.1
1994	January	167.1	91.8	84.6	6.3	2.5	194.9
	February	161.7	92.7	82.8	6.5	2.9	189.2
	March	160.4	91.8	83.2	6.0	3.2	190.0
	April	153.4	88.2	79.7	5.5	2.8	180.2
	May	160.7	89.0	81.1	5.3	3.3	189.7
	June	165.7	93.7	85.4	4.9	3.3	194.5
	July	152.6	88.7	80.7	5.1	3.4	178.3
	August	158.4	90.0	84.5	5.0	3.6	187.4
	September	159.9	90.4	87.1	4.2	3.8	188.8
	October	154.4	88.4	82.0	4.2	4.0	181.8
	November	158.6	89.4	85.6	5.6	4.5	190.1
	December	153.5	87.0	79.5	6.0	3.9	184.0
	All 1994	1906.4	1082.1	996.4	64.6	41.1	2249.0
1995	January	157.7	92.5	85.1	5.7	4.1	189.5
	February	162.4	94.7	86.0	6.1	4.2	194.4
	March	160.5	93.0	84.6	6.2	3.8	193.3
	April	152.8	92.3	81.9	6.0	4.2	181.8
	May	162.1	95.7	85.2	6.0	3.8	194.2
	June	163.4	93.6	83.9	5.1	3.9	192.5
	July	158.7	94.3	82.3	6.3	4.6	187.6
	August	162.6	94.5	86.6	5.4	3.9	192.5
	September	159.4	93.0	82.9	4.9	3.6	189.2
	October	167.3	97.1	89.9	5.3	4.0	196.8
	November	166.1	95.6	86.9	5.8	4.2	197.0
	December	165.1	96.2	87.2	6.1	3.8	197.7
	All 1995	1938.1	1132.3	1022.4	68.9	48.0	2306.6
1996	January	160.4	96.2	83.9	7.1	4.0	192.7
	February	170.3	101.8	88.3	6.3	3.5	203.1
	March	162.0	98.0	86.1	7.0	3.7	193.7
	April	175.4	105.6	91.1	7.7	3.7	207.0
	May	169.2	104.9	87.8	8.1	3.7	204.1
	June	169.0	104.2	89.4	7.7	3.8	202.0
	July	170.1	103.5	88.4	7.0	3.6	199.2
	August	167.1	103.2	88.1	7.0	3.6	198.9
	September	160.7	103.7	85.5	6.8	7.2	196.2
	October	178.1	110.2	90.4	7.4	2.4	209.9
	November	167.6	106.5	87.3	7.8	3.1	200.2
	December	168.4	108.2	90.4	9.7	3.3	203.2
	All 1996	2018.3	1246.1	1056.7	89.6	45.5	2410.1

1 Seasonal adjustment constrained to equal actual annual totals.

Table 14 Motor Vehicles registered for the first time: Historic series: 1951-1985

For detail on years 1986 - 1996 see table 10

Thousands

Year	Private and light goods [1]	Goods vehicles [1]	Motor cycles scooters and mopeds [2]	Public transport vehicles [3]	Special machines etc [4]	Other vehicles [5,6]	All vehicles
1951	136.2	84.5	133.4	7.8	34.4	17.6	413.9
1952	187.6	81.8	132.5	5.4	35.3	16.0	458.6
1953	295.1	97.2	138.6	5.0	33.5	14.1	583.5
1954	386.4	109.6	164.6	5.5	35.2	17.1	718.4
1955	500.9	153.5	185.2	5.6	39.2	22.1	906.5
1956	399.7	148.0	142.8	5.1	31.9	23.3	750.8
1957	425.4	140.5	206.1	5.0	39.8	19.9	836.7
1958	555.3	172.6	182.7	4.9	47.2	18.9	981.6
1959	645.6	191.7	331.8	5.1	49.0	29.7	1,252.9
1960	805.0	225.9	256.7	6.4	42.5	32.9	1,369.4
1961	742.8	220.2	212.4	6.1	46.4	31.4	1,259.3
1962	784.7	192.3	140.2	5.5	42.8	26.7	1,192.2
1963	1,008.6	206.4	165.5	6.4	47.9	31.2	1,466.0
1964	1,190.6	229.3	205.1	6.5	46.1	33.6	1,711.2
1965	1,122.5	229.4	150.9	6.8	45.4	45.7	1,600.7
1966	1,065.4	227.2	109.4	6.8	48.4	36.4	1,493.6
1967	1,116.7	221.5	137.7	6.5	53.9	38.9	1,575.2
1968	1,116.9	231.7	112.0	7.1	57.0	37.2	1,561.9
1969	987.4	239.6	85.4	7.1	49.3	33.0	1,401.8
1969	1,133.2	93.8	85.4	7.1	49.3	33.0	1,401.8
1970	1,248.1	85.2	104.9	7.7	48.8	30.2	1,524.9
1971	1,462.1	74.2	127.9	9.5	37.9	30.0	1,741.6
1972	1,854.8	74.9	152.5	9.8	47.6	44.1	2,183.7
1973	1,851.3	82.7	193.6	10.0	49.7	43.0	2,230.3
1974	1,399.6	68.0	189.8	7.8	45.6	39.6	1,750.4
1975	1,317.2	67.0	264.8	7.8	48.5	44.6	1,749.9
1976	1,401.8	63.9	270.6	8.7	51.8	41.2	1,838.0
1977	1,445.0	68.8	251.3	8.8	48.3	39.8	1,862.0
1978	1,745.8	79.8	225.3	9.1	50.0	41.4	2,151.4
1979	1,891.5	91.3	285.9	9.1	47.7	44.4	2,369.9
1980	1,679.2	74.7	312.7	8.8	36.7	43.5	2,155.6
1980	1,699.2	54.9	312.7	8.8	36.7	43.5	2,155.8
1981	1,643.6	39.9	271.9	7.5	32.6	34.8	2,030.3
1982	1,745.5	41.2	231.6	7.1	41.2	39.6	2,103.9
1983	1,989.1	46.6	174.5	7.3	42.1	47.9	2,307.5
1984	1,932.6	49.6	145.2	7.2	40.1	64.2	2,238.9
1985	2,029.5	51.7	125.8	6.8	40.1	55.4	2,309.3

1 From 1969 onwards registrations for the new October 1982 taxation
   classes have been estimated. See Notes. Figures for 1951- 1969 refer to
   previous classes. From 1980 onwards figures relate to the October 1990 taxation classes
2 Includes scooters and mopeds.
3 Includes taxis but excludes tram cars.
4 Includes trench diggers, mobile cranes, etc but excludes agricultural
   tractors on exempt licences.
5 Includes crown and exempt vehicles, three wheelers, pedestrian
   controlled vehicles, and showmens' goods vehicles.
6 Excludes vehicles officially registered by the armed forces.

Table 15 Goods vehicle stock at end of year: 1986 - 1996

Thousands

Year	Rigid vehicles	Articulated vehicles Not over 28 tonnes	Articulated vehicles 28-37 tonnes	Articulated vehicles over 37 tonnes	Articulated vehicles All	All vehicles
1986 [1]	341	13	46	34	93	435
1987	346	14	43	41	98	444
1988	357	14	40	51	105	462
1989	368	14	36	60	110	478
1990 [1]	353	14	30	63	106	460
1991	330	13	26	61	100	430
1992	316	13	23	63	99	415
1993	313	12	21	64	98	410
1994	312	13	20	71	103	416
1995	311	13	18	76	107	418
1996	311	13	17	79	110	421

1 The analysis was delayed until the end of January the following year. Figures therefore include vehicles
newly registered (about 3,000 in 1987 and 2,000 in 1991) or scrapped during the following January.

Trailers - analysis by axle type[1]

Thousands

National totals	1 axle	2 axle	3 axle	4 axle	5 axle	Total
First / Annual tests in 1992	13.1	132.2	75.6	0.1	-	221.0
First / Annual tests in 1993	12.0	128.5	83.7	0.1	-	224.3
First / Annual tests in 1994	11.1	122.3	92.1	0.1	-	225.6
First / Annual tests in 1995	10.2	115.1	101.2	0.1	-	226.7

1 This table is derived from Vehicle Inspectorate data on the number of trailers tested.
Total stock at the end of 1991 was estimated to be between 230 and 240 thousand trailers.

Table 16 Goods vehicle stock: by gross weight and axle configuration: 1996

Thousands

Tractor	Trailer	Over / Not over	3.5 t / 7.5 t	7.5 t / 12 t	12 t / 16 t	16 t / 20 t	20 t / 24 t	24 t / 28 t	28 t / 32 t	32 t / 33 t	33 t / 37 t	37 t / 38 t	38 t	All weights
Rigid vehicles														
2 Axle			153.1	15.7	21.9	72.6	-	0.0	0.0	-	0.0	0.0	0.0	263.2
3 Axle			0.1	0.1	0.1	0.4	4.6	23.5	0.0	0.0	0.0	0.0	0.0	28.8
4 Axle			0.1	-	0.2	0.1	-	0.1	18.4	0.0	0.0	0.0	0.0	18.9
All rigid			153.3	15.7	22.2	73.1	4.7	23.6	18.4	-	0.0	0.0	0.0	311.0
Articulated vehicles														
2 Axle	2 Axle		0.0	0.0	0.0	0.1	0.4	3.6	-	-	-	-	0.0	4.2
	3 Axle		0.0	0.0	0.0	-	0.1	0.5	0.2	0.7	1.3	43.4	0.0	46.1
	Any		0.2	-	-	1.1	0.8	5.6	2.1	11.8	0.1	0.8	-	22.5
All 2 Axle			0.2	-	-	1.3	1.3	9.7	2.4	12.5	1.3	44.2	-	72.9
3 Axle	2 Axle		-	-	0.0	0.0	0.0	-	-	0.3	0.1	-	-	0.5
	3 Axle		0.0	0.0	-	-	-	-	-	0.1	0.1	19.8	0.7	20.7
	Any		0.1	-	-	0.1	0.1	0.4	0.1	0.1	-	14.1	0.6	15.6
All 3 Axle			0.1	-	-	0.1	0.1	0.5	0.1	0.5	0.2	34.0	1.2	36.8
2 & 3 Axl	2 Axle		-	-	0.0	0.1	0.4	3.6	-	0.3	0.1	0.1	-	4.7
	3 Axle		0.0	0.0	-	-	0.1	0.5	0.2	0.7	1.3	63.2	0.7	66.8
	Any		0.2	-	0.1	1.2	0.9	6.0	2.2	11.9	0.1	14.9	0.6	38.1
All articulated			0.2	-	0.1	1.3	1.4	10.2	2.4	13.0	1.5	78.2	1.2	109.6

Table 17 Goods vehicle stock: by taxation[1] group and axle configuration: 1996

Thousands

| | Rigid vehicles | | | | Articulated vehicles | | | | | | | | | | |
| | | | | | 2 axle tractor | | | | 3 axle tractor | | | | | |
Taxation class(es)	2 axle	3 axle	4 axle	All	2 axle trailer	3 axle trailer	any trailer	All	2 axle trailer	3 axle trailer	any trailer	All	All	All
General goods														
1 HGV	250.9	26.6	18.7	296.2	4.2	46.1	22.3	72.6	0.5	20.7	15.5	36.7	109.4	405.5
2 Trailer HGV	5.0	1.9	-	7.0	0.0	0.0	0.0	0.0	0.0	0.0	-	-	-	7.0
Others														
16 Small Island	0.2	-	-	0.2	0.0	-	-	-	0.0	0.0	-	-	0.1	0.2
Electric classes	3.1	-	-	3.1	0.0	0.0	-	-	0.0	0.0	-	-	-	3.1
Crown vehicles	0.4	-	-	0.4	0.0	-	-	-	0.0	0.0	-	-	-	0.4
Exempt not crown	3.7	0.3	0.1	4.1	-	-	0.2	0.2	-	-	-	-	0.2	4.3
Total	263.2	28.8	18.9	311.0	4.2	46.1	22.5	72.9	0.5	20.7	15.6	36.8	109.6	420.6

1 Only vehicles in these taxation groups greater than 3500kg gross vehicle weight, and with goods vehicle body type.

Table 18 Rigid goods vehicle stock: by gross vehicle weight and type of body: 1996

Thousands

Body type	Over Not over	3.5 t 7.5 t	7.5 t 12 t	12 t 16 t	16 t 20 t	20 t 24 t	24 t 28 t	28 t 32 t	32 t ___	All weights
Rigid vehicles										
Panel Van		6.2	0.1	0.1	0.2	-	-	0.0	0.0	6.5
Box Van		59.1	6.4	7.5	24.2	1.0	1.3	0.1	0.0	99.6
Car Derived Van		0.1	-	0.1	-	-	-	-	0.0	0.2
Light Van		0.7	-	0.1	0.1	-	-	-	0.0	0.9
Pick-Up		0.2	-	-	-	-	-	0.0	0.0	0.2
Motor Caravan		0.2	-	-	-	0.0	-	0.0	0.0	0.2
Van/Side Windows		0.3	-	-	0.1	-	-	0.0	0.0	0.4
Light Goods		0.1	-	-	-	-	-	-	0.0	0.2
Pantechnicon		0.4	0.1	0.2	0.4	-	-	-	0.0	1.0
Luton Van		2.6	0.3	0.4	0.3	-	-	-	0.0	3.5
Insulated Van		5.7	1.1	0.9	3.4	0.2	0.4	-	0.0	11.7
Glass Carrier		0.2	-	0.1	0.1	-	-	0.0	0.0	0.4
Specially Fitted Van		0.6	0.1	0.1	0.2	-	-	-	0.0	1.1
Van		3.1	0.2	0.4	0.4	-	-	-	0.0	4.2
Livestock Carrier		2.2	0.3	0.2	0.3	-	0.1	-	0.0	3.2
Float		3.1	-	-	-	-	-	0.0	0.0	3.2
Flat Lorry		10.4	1.7	1.8	7.6	0.8	2.1	1.0	0.0	25.4
Dropside Lorry		12.4	1.0	1.5	4.7	0.1	0.5	0.1	0.0	20.4
Tipper		22.7	1.1	2.4	7.4	0.2	7.1	11.9	0.0	52.8
Low Loader		0.1	-	-	0.1	-	-	-	0.0	0.2
Truck		0.8	0.1	0.1	0.2	-	0.1	-	0.0	1.3
Breakdown Truck		0.8	0.1	0.1	0.1	-	-	-	0.0	1.0
Tanker		0.3	0.2	0.3	2.9	0.1	2.3	0.9	0.0	7.0
Solid Bulk Carrier		-	-	-	-	-	0.1	0.1	0.0	0.2
Concrete Mixer		-	-	0.2	0.2	-	2.7	0.1	0.0	3.3
Mobile Plant		0.2	-	-	0.1	-	-	-	0.0	0.3
Car Transporter		0.6	0.1	0.1	1.0	0.1	-	-	0.0	1.9
Refuse Disposal		0.4	0.2	0.1	3.1	1.1	3.1	1.2	0.0	9.2
Goods		4.8	0.6	0.8	3.4	0.2	0.8	0.6	-	11.2
Front Dumper		0.1	-	-	-	0.0	-	-	0.0	0.1
Skip Loader		0.9	0.1	0.2	4.7	0.1	0.6	0.6	0.0	7.2
Special Mobile Unit		0.2	-	-	0.1	-	-	-	0.0	0.3
Landrover/Jeep		0.1	-	-	-	-	0.0	-	0.0	0.1
Airport Support Unit		0.1	-	-	0.1	0.0	-	-	0.0	0.3
Skeletal Goods		0.2	0.1	0.1	0.2	-	0.1	-	0.0	0.6
Other or not known		13.8	1.8	4.3	7.3	0.5	2.1	1.7	-	31.6
Total		153.3	15.7	22.2	73.1	4.7	23.6	18.4	-	311.0

Table 19 Goods vehicle stock: by GVW [1] and year of 1st registration: 1996

Thousands

Year of first registration	Over Not over	3.5 t 7.5 t	7.5 t 12 t	12 t 16 t	16 t 20 t	20 t 24 t	24 t 28 t	28 t 32 t	32 t 33 t	33 t 37 t	37 t 38 t	38 t	All weights
Rigid vehicles													
Pre-1986		24.0	2.6	3.6	8.5	0.4	3.0	1.5		0.0		0.0	43.7
1986		8.1	0.9	1.3	3.7	0.2	1.2	0.9		-		0.0	16.1
1987		10.6	1.0	1.8	5.0	0.2	1.6	1.3		0.0		0.0	21.6
1988		14.3	1.3	2.1	7.5	0.3	2.3	2.1		0.0		0.0	29.9
1989		15.6	1.6	2.2	8.2	0.5	2.8	2.6		0.0		0.0	33.5
1990		12.6	1.4	1.9	6.4	0.4	1.9	1.3		0.0		0.0	26.0
1991		9.0	1.0	1.4	4.1	0.3	1.2	0.7		0.0		0.0	17.8
1992		9.3	1.1	1.4	4.2	0.3	1.1	0.7		0.0		0.0	18.0
1993		9.7	1.3	1.5	5.1	0.3	1.4	1.1		0.0		0.0	20.4
1994		12.1	1.0	1.5	6.2	0.5	2.1	2.3		0.0		0.0	25.7
1995		14.1	1.2	1.7	7.4	0.7	2.6	2.3		0.0		0.0	30.0
1996		13.7	1.3	1.7	6.8	0.7	2.5	1.7		0.0		0.0	28.4
All years		153.3	15.7	22.2	73.1	4.7	23.6	18.4		-		0.0	311.0
Articulated vehicles													
Pre-1986		0.1		0.2	0.1	0.7	0.1	1.0	0.1	3.8		-	6.1
1986		-		0.1	0.1	0.4	-	0.5	-	2.2		0.0	3.4
1987		-		0.1	0.1	0.7	0.1	0.7	-	3.8		-	5.4
1988		-		0.2	0.1	0.8	0.1	1.2	0.1	6.2		-	8.7
1989		-		0.3	0.1	1.0	0.1	1.2	0.1	7.5		-	10.3
1990		-		0.1	0.1	0.8	0.1	0.9	-	5.1		-	7.3
1991		-		0.1	0.1	0.7	0.1	0.7	0.1	3.9		-	5.8
1992		-		0.1	0.1	0.8	0.2	0.8	0.1	4.8		0.1	7.0
1993		-		0.1	0.2	0.9	0.2	1.2	0.2	6.8		-	9.6
1994		-		-	0.1	1.1	0.5	1.7	0.2	9.6		0.1	13.5
1995		-		0.1	0.2	1.5	0.5	1.4	0.3	12.4		0.5	16.8
1996		-		0.1	0.1	1.0	0.3	1.6	0.2	12.0		0.5	15.8
All years		0.3		1.3	1.4	10.2	2.4	13.0	1.5	78.2		1.2	109.6
Rigid and articulated vehicles													
Pre-1986		24.1	2.6	3.6	8.7	0.5	3.7	1.6	1.0	0.1	3.8	-	49.8
1986		8.1	0.9	1.3	3.8	0.2	1.5	0.9	0.5	-	2.2	0.0	19.5
1987		10.7	1.0	1.8	5.1	0.3	2.2	1.4	0.7	-	3.8	-	27.0
1988		14.3	1.3	2.1	7.6	0.5	3.1	2.2	1.2	0.1	6.2	-	38.6
1989		15.6	1.6	2.2	8.4	0.6	3.8	2.7	1.2	0.1	7.5	-	43.8
1990		12.7	1.4	1.9	6.5	0.5	2.7	1.5	0.9	-	5.1	-	33.2
1991		9.1	1.0	1.4	4.3	0.4	1.9	0.9	0.7	0.1	3.9	-	23.6
1992		9.3	1.1	1.4	4.2	0.5	1.8	0.8	0.8	0.1	4.8	0.1	25.0
1993		9.7	1.3	1.5	5.2	0.5	2.2	1.3	1.2	0.2	6.8	-	29.9
1994		12.1	1.0	1.6	6.2	0.6	3.1	2.8	1.7	0.2	9.6	0.1	39.2
1995		14.1	1.2	1.7	7.5	0.8	4.1	2.8	1.4	0.3	12.4	0.5	46.8
1996		13.7	1.3	1.7	6.9	0.8	3.5	2.0	1.6	0.2	12.0	0.5	44.2
All years		153.5	15.8	22.3	74.4	6.1	33.8	20.9	13.0	1.5	78.2	1.2	420.6

1 GVW: Gross vehicle weight.

Table 20 Rigid goods vehicle stock: by year of 1st registration and type of body: 1996

Thousands

Body type	1986 & before	1987	1988	1989	1990	1991	1992	1993	1994	1995	1996	All years
Rigid vehicles												
Panel Van	0.6	0.4	0.5	0.7	0.7	0.6	0.4	0.4	0.6	0.7	0.8	6.5
Box Van	10.7	5.6	8.8	9.9	8.0	6.2	7.2	8.7	10.3	12.5	11.7	99.6
Car Derived Van	0.1	-	-	-	-	-	-	-	-	-	-	0.2
Light Van	0.2	0.1	0.1	0.1	0.1	0.1	0.1	-	-	-	0.1	0.9
Pick-Up	0.1	-	-	-	-	-	-	-	-	-	-	0.2
Motor Caravan	0.1	-	-	-	-	-	-	-	-	-	-	0.2
Van/Side Windows	0.1	0.1	0.1	-	-	-	-	-	-	-	-	0.4
Light Goods	0.1	-	-	-	-	-	-	-	-	-	-	0.2
Pantechnicon	0.4	0.1	0.1	0.1	-	0.1	-	0.1	0.1	-	-	1.0
Luton Van	1.4	0.3	0.4	0.4	0.3	0.2	0.1	0.1	0.1	0.2	0.1	3.5
Insulated Van	1.0	0.5	0.7	0.9	1.0	1.0	1.2	1.1	1.2	1.5	1.6	11.7
Glass Carrier	-	-	-	-	-	-	-	-	-	0.1	-	0.4
Specially Fitted Van	0.3	0.1	0.1	0.2	0.1	-	0.1	-	0.1	-	-	1.1
Van	1.6	0.5	0.4	0.3	0.3	0.2	0.2	0.2	0.1	0.2	0.3	4.2
Livestock Carrier	1.8	0.2	0.2	0.3	0.2	0.1	0.1	0.1	0.1	0.1	0.1	3.2
Float	2.3	0.2	0.2	0.2	0.1	0.1	0.1	-	-	-	-	3.2
Flat Lorry	9.0	2.3	2.9	2.9	1.9	0.9	0.8	0.8	1.1	1.3	1.3	25.4
Dropside Lorry	4.8	1.5	2.2	2.5	1.7	0.9	0.9	1.2	1.5	1.7	1.6	20.4
Tipper	11.1	3.7	5.6	6.8	4.3	2.7	2.1	2.9	4.8	4.9	3.8	52.8
Low Loader	0.1	-	-	-	-	-	-	-	-	-	-	0.2
Truck	0.5	0.1	0.1	0.1	0.1	0.1	0.1	-	-	0.1	0.1	1.3
Breakdown Truck	0.3	0.1	0.1	0.1	0.1	-	-	-	-	0.1	0.1	1.0
Tanker	1.4	0.6	0.8	0.7	0.6	0.6	0.4	0.4	0.4	0.6	0.5	7.0
Solid Bulk Carrier	0.1	-	-	-	-	-	-	-	-	-	-	0.2
Concrete Mixer	0.3	0.3	0.5	0.5	0.3	0.1	0.1	0.1	0.2	0.5	0.4	3.3
Mobile Plant	0.1	-	-	-	-	-	-	-	-	-	-	0.3
Car Transporter	0.2	0.1	0.2	0.3	0.3	0.1	0.1	0.1	0.1	0.2	0.2	1.9
Refuse Disposal	0.8	0.6	0.8	0.9	0.9	0.7	0.7	0.8	0.9	1.1	1.1	9.2
Goods	3.4	1.1	1.4	1.7	1.2	0.6	0.7	0.2	0.1	0.2	0.6	11.2
Front Dumper	-	-	-	-	-	-	-	-	-	-	-	0.1
Skip Loader	1.6	0.6	0.8	0.9	0.7	0.3	0.2	0.3	0.5	0.7	0.6	7.2
Special Mobile Unit	0.1	-	-	-	-	-	-	-	-	-	-	0.3
Landrover/Jeep	-	-	-	-	-	-	0.0	-	-	-	-	0.1
Airport Support Unit	0.1	-	-	-	-	-	-	-	-	-	-	0.3
Skeletal Goods	-	-	-	-	-	-	0.1	0.1	0.1	0.1	0.1	0.6
Other or not known	5.1	2.4	2.6	3.1	2.8	2.0	2.1	2.5	3.1	3.1	2.8	31.6
Total	59.8	21.6	29.9	33.5	26.0	17.8	18.0	20.4	25.7	30.0	28.4	311.0

Table 21 Goods vehicle stock: by county, region and axle configuration: 1996

Thousands

Country/region/local authority	Articulated vehicles								All
	2 axle tractor				3 axle tractor				
	2 axle trailer	3 axle trailer	any trailer	All	2 axle trailer	3 axle trailer	any trailer	All	All
Great Britain	4.22	46.11	22.53	72.85	0.50	20.70	15.58	36.77	109.63
Vehicle Under Disposal	0.03	0.39	0.26	0.69	0.01	0.23	0.15	0.38	1.07
County Unknown	0.05	0.38	0.18	0.61	-	0.16	0.14	0.30	0.90
England	3.75	39.62	20.28	63.65	0.45	17.80	13.39	31.64	95.30
Northern Region	0.22	3.27	0.69	4.18	0.01	0.98	0.94	1.93	6.10
Cleveland	0.02	0.81	0.12	0.96	0.00	0.08	0.15	0.23	1.19
Hartlepool UA	-	0.05	0.02	0.07	0.00	0.01	0.01	0.02	0.08
Redcar & Cleveland UA	-	0.20	0.01	0.21	0.00	0.02	0.05	0.06	0.27
Middlesbrough UA	-	0.10	0.02	0.12	0.00	0.01	0.03	0.04	0.16
Stockton-On-Tees UA	0.02	0.47	0.08	0.57	0.00	0.05	0.07	0.11	0.68
Cumbria	0.05	1.09	0.13	1.27	-	0.38	0.34	0.72	1.99
Durham	0.07	0.68	0.13	0.88	-	0.19	0.22	0.42	1.29
Northumberland	0.03	0.31	0.07	0.41	0.00	0.11	0.10	0.21	0.62
Tyne & Wear	0.05	0.38	0.24	0.67	-	0.23	0.12	0.35	1.02
Yorkshire & Humberside Region	0.34	5.88	2.10	8.32	0.05	2.54	2.04	4.63	12.95
Humberside	0.06	1.48	0.18	1.71	-	1.02	0.48	1.51	3.22
East Riding of Yorkshire UA	0.01	0.56	0.06	0.63	-	0.35	0.15	0.49	1.12
Kingston Upon Hull UA	0.01	0.20	0.07	0.27	-	0.26	0.07	0.33	0.61
North Lincolnshire UA	0.03	0.47	0.03	0.53	-	0.23	0.14	0.37	0.91
North East Lincolnshire UA	-	0.26	0.02	0.28	0.00	0.18	0.12	0.31	0.59
North Yorkshire	0.05	1.40	0.33	1.77	-	0.43	0.30	0.73	2.50
York UA	0.01	0.04	0.03	0.08	-	0.03	0.08	0.11	0.19
Rest of North Yorkshire	0.03	1.37	0.30	1.70	-	0.40	0.22	0.62	2.32
South Yorkshire	0.09	0.90	0.52	1.51	0.01	0.37	0.55	0.93	2.44
West Yorkshire	0.15	2.10	1.08	3.33	0.04	0.72	0.71	1.47	4.79
East Midland Region	0.47	3.70	2.33	6.49	0.04	2.09	1.57	3.69	10.19
Derbyshire	0.04	0.71	0.41	1.16	0.01	0.32	0.33	0.66	1.81
Leicestershire	0.05	0.69	0.21	0.95	-	0.26	0.16	0.42	1.37
Lincolnshire	0.04	0.86	0.20	1.10	0.01	0.89	0.40	1.30	2.40
Northamptonshire	0.29	0.78	1.07	2.13	0.01	0.37	0.39	0.76	2.89
Nottinghamshire	0.06	0.66	0.44	1.16	0.01	0.26	0.28	0.55	1.71
East Anglia Region	0.15	3.50	1.18	4.83	0.05	2.02	1.63	3.71	8.53
Cambridgeshire	0.07	1.03	0.49	1.59	0.01	0.44	0.23	0.68	2.27
Norfolk	0.02	0.98	0.28	1.28	0.01	0.70	0.35	1.07	2.35
Suffolk	0.05	1.49	0.41	1.95	0.04	0.88	1.05	1.97	3.92
South Eastern Region	0.87	10.26	5.50	16.63	0.11	4.40	2.50	7.01	23.64
Bedfordshire	0.02	0.36	0.15	0.53	0.01	0.19	0.09	0.29	0.82
Berkshire	0.08	0.52	0.54	1.14	-	0.21	0.11	0.32	1.46
Buckinghamshire	0.09	2.04	0.47	2.60	-	0.41	0.36	0.77	3.37
East Sussex	0.01	0.12	0.05	0.18	0.00	0.10	0.03	0.13	0.32
Essex	0.06	1.39	0.43	1.87	0.02	0.76	0.33	1.11	2.98
Greater London	0.34	2.05	2.05	4.45	0.06	0.85	0.67	1.58	6.02
Hampshire	0.09	0.68	0.45	1.22	0.01	0.36	0.18	0.54	1.77
Hertfordshire	0.02	0.90	0.60	1.53	-	0.27	0.14	0.42	1.95
Isle of Wight UA	-	0.01	0.01	0.01	0.00	-	0.04	0.04	0.05
Kent	0.08	1.06	0.25	1.39	0.01	0.90	0.31	1.22	2.61
Oxfordshire	0.02	0.53	0.24	0.79	0.00	0.09	0.09	0.18	0.97
Surrey	0.02	0.47	0.15	0.64	-	0.14	0.06	0.20	0.84
West Sussex	0.05	0.14	0.10	0.28	-	0.12	0.08	0.21	0.49
South Western Region	0.23	1.96	0.66	2.85	0.02	0.74	0.52	1.27	4.12
Avon	-	0.01	0.01	0.02	0.00	0.02	0.01	0.03	0.05
Bristol UA	-	0.02	-	0.03	0.00	0.01	0.04	0.05	0.07
North Somerset UA	0.01	0.05	0.01	0.07	0.00	0.01	0.01	0.02	0.09
Bath & North East Somerset UA	0.01	0.13	0.02	0.16	-	0.02	0.03	0.05	0.21
South Gloucestershire UA	-	0.03	0.02	0.05	-	0.01	0.02	0.03	0.08
Cornwall	0.03	0.04	0.04	0.11	-	0.04	0.01	0.05	0.16
Devonshire	0.02	0.15	0.03	0.19	-	0.05	0.06	0.11	0.30
Dorset	0.01	0.02	0.01	0.05	0.00	0.02	0.01	0.03	0.07
Gloucestershire	0.02	0.21	0.03	0.25	-	0.08	0.07	0.15	0.40
Somerset	0.00	0.04	-	0.04	0.00	0.06	0.01	0.07	0.11
Wiltshire	0.02	0.24	0.20	0.45	0.01	0.06	0.05	0.12	0.57

Table 21 (Cont'd)

Thousands

Country/region/local authority	Rigid vehicles				All goods vehicles
	2 axle	3 axle	4 axle	All	
Great Britain	263.23	28.81	18.92	310.96	420.59
Vehicle Under Disposal	3.92	0.24	0.15	4.31	5.38
County Unknown	2.48	0.24	0.17	2.88	3.79
England	225.41	23.79	16.13	265.32	360.62
Northern Region	10.17	1.29	0.87	12.34	18.44
Cleveland	1.42	0.18	0.08	1.67	2.86
Hartlepool UA	0.19	0.05	0.02	0.25	0.33
Redcar & Cleveland UA	0.22	0.02	0.01	0.25	0.52
Middlesbrough UA	0.24	0.03	-	0.27	0.43
Stockton-On-Tees UA	0.78	0.08	0.05	0.90	1.58
Cumbria	2.16	0.36	0.17	2.69	4.68
Durham	1.89	0.28	0.23	2.40	3.70
Northumberland	0.98	0.13	0.16	1.27	1.89
Tyne & Wear	3.73	0.35	0.22	4.31	5.32
Yorkshire & Humberside Region	24.78	2.61	1.56	28.95	41.90
Humberside	2.84	0.43	0.24	3.51	6.73
East Riding of Yorkshire UA	1.01	0.21	0.14	1.36	2.47
Kingston Upon Hull UA	0.94	0.11	0.03	1.08	1.69
North Lincolnshire UA	0.55	0.07	0.05	0.67	1.58
North East Lincolnshire UA	0.34	0.04	0.02	0.40	0.99
North Yorkshire	4.46	0.59	0.36	5.41	7.91
York UA	0.75	0.06	0.03	0.84	1.03
Rest of North Yorkshire	3.71	0.53	0.33	4.57	6.88
South Yorkshire	6.30	0.61	0.45	7.36	9.80
West Yorkshire	11.19	0.98	0.51	12.67	17.47
East Midland Region	21.53	2.50	1.89	25.92	36.11
Derbyshire	5.28	0.71	0.59	6.57	8.39
Leicestershire	4.24	0.48	0.52	5.24	6.61
Lincolnshire	2.72	0.36	0.25	3.33	5.74
Northamptonshire	4.61	0.30	0.15	5.06	7.95
Nottinghamshire	4.68	0.66	0.38	5.72	7.43
East Anglia Region	10.28	1.14	0.85	12.27	20.80
Cambridgeshire	3.61	0.43	0.35	4.38	6.65
Norfolk	3.32	0.40	0.30	4.02	6.37
Suffolk	3.35	0.32	0.19	3.87	7.78
South Eastern Region	67.62	6.18	5.14	78.95	102.58
Bedfordshire	2.41	0.24	0.39	3.03	3.85
Berkshire	4.34	0.27	0.17	4.78	6.24
Buckinghamshire	3.94	0.38	0.31	4.63	8.00
East Sussex	2.06	0.12	0.09	2.28	2.59
Essex	6.26	0.76	0.74	7.75	10.73
Greater London	22.49	1.65	1.60	25.74	31.76
Hampshire	5.83	0.51	0.41	6.74	8.51
Hertfordshire	4.64	0.56	0.39	5.59	7.54
Isle of Wight UA	0.32	0.03	0.01	0.36	0.42
Kent	5.39	0.61	0.46	6.46	9.07
Oxfordshire	2.28	0.32	0.22	2.81	3.78
Surrey	5.34	0.54	0.19	6.07	6.91
West Sussex	2.34	0.17	0.18	2.69	3.18
South Western Region	11.72	1.43	0.98	14.13	18.25
Avon	0.38	0.03	0.07	0.48	0.53
Bristol UA	0.30	0.04	0.01	0.35	0.42
North Somerset UA	0.14	0.01	0.01	0.16	0.25
Bath & North East Somerset UA	0.40	0.03	0.06	0.48	0.69
South Gloucestershire UA	0.58	0.06	0.04	0.68	0.76
Cornwall	0.53	0.05	0.05	0.63	0.79
Devonshire	1.42	0.07	0.06	1.55	1.85
Dorset	0.40	0.04	0.01	0.45	0.52
Gloucestershire	0.96	0.16	0.07	1.18	1.58
Somerset	0.40	0.06	0.06	0.52	0.63
Wiltshire	0.71	0.10	0.13	0.95	1.51

Table 21 (Cont'd)

Thousands

| | Articulated vehicles | | | | | | | | |
| | 2 axle tractor | | | | 3 axle tractor | | | | |
Country/region/local authority	2 axle trailer	3 axle trailer	any trailer	All	2 axle trailer	3 axle trailer	any trailer	All	All
West Midland Region	0.69	4.13	3.30	8.12	0.11	2.11	1.47	3.69	11.81
Hereford & Worcestershire	0.04	0.46	0.45	0.95	0.01	0.30	0.22	0.53	1.48
Salop	0.05	0.43	0.15	0.62	-	0.31	0.14	0.45	1.07
Staffordshire	0.21	0.98	1.13	2.32	0.01	0.50	0.44	0.95	3.26
Warwickshire	0.12	0.28	0.30	0.70	0.01	0.17	0.14	0.32	1.01
West Midlands	0.27	2.00	1.27	3.54	0.08	0.83	0.52	1.44	4.98
North Western Region	0.74	5.46	3.52	9.71	0.06	2.04	2.50	4.60	14.31
Cheshire	0.16	1.38	0.73	2.27	0.01	0.46	0.44	0.91	3.18
Greater Manchester	0.33	1.99	1.63	3.95	0.03	0.73	1.05	1.81	5.77
Lancashire	0.16	1.05	0.68	1.89	0.01	0.50	0.64	1.15	3.04
Merseyside	0.09	1.04	0.47	1.60	0.01	0.36	0.36	0.73	2.33
Scotland	0.00	0.05	0.01	0.06	0.00	-	0.02	0.02	0.08
Aberdeen City UA	0.01	0.06	0.19	0.26	0.00	0.02	0.03	0.05	0.30
Aberdeenshire UA	-	0.17	0.06	0.22	0.00	0.05	0.14	0.19	0.41
Angus UA	-	0.21	0.04	0.26	-	0.06	0.08	0.14	0.40
Argyll & Bute UA	0.01	0.16	0.15	0.32	-	0.07	0.10	0.18	0.50
The Scottish Borders UA	0.01	0.18	0.02	0.20	-	0.09	0.07	0.16	0.36
Clackmannanshire UA	0.00	0.02	-	0.02	0.00	-	0.01	0.01	0.03
West Dunbartonshire UA	-	0.04	-	0.04	0.00	0.02	0.01	0.03	0.07
Dumfries & Galloway UA	-	0.11	0.01	0.12	0.00	0.02	0.08	0.10	0.21
City of Dundee UA	-	0.03	0.01	0.04	0.00	0.02	0.06	0.08	0.12
East Ayrshire UA	0.01	0.24	0.15	0.40	0.00	0.19	0.10	0.28	0.69
East Dunbartonshire UA	0.00	-	0.01	0.01	0.00	0.01	0.01	0.01	0.02
East Lothian UA	0.01	0.10	0.02	0.13	0.00	0.08	0.01	0.09	0.22
East Renfrewshire UA	-	0.07	0.04	0.12	-	0.03	0.19	0.23	0.34
City of Endinburgh UA	-	-	0.01	0.02	0.00	0.01	0.01	0.02	0.03
Falkirk UA	-	0.13	0.02	0.15	-	0.03	0.02	0.04	0.20
Fife UA	0.01	0.15	0.05	0.20	-	0.11	0.04	0.15	0.35
City of Glasgow UA	-	0.06	0.01	0.07	0.00	0.04	0.02	0.06	0.13
Highland UA	0.01	0.17	0.05	0.22	0.00	0.05	0.05	0.10	0.33
Inverclyde UA	-	0.01	0.01	0.03	0.00	0.03	0.01	0.03	0.06
Midlothian UA	0.23	1.96	0.66	2.85	0.02	0.74	0.52	1.27	4.12
Moray UA	-	0.01	0.01	0.02	0.00	0.02	0.01	0.03	0.05
North Ayrshire UA	-	0.02	-	0.03	0.00	0.01	0.04	0.05	0.07
North Lanarkshire UA	0.01	0.05	0.01	0.07	0.00	0.01	0.01	0.02	0.09
Orkney Islands UA	0.01	0.13	0.02	0.16	-	0.02	0.03	0.05	0.21
Perth & Kinross UA	-	0.03	0.02	0.05	-	0.01	0.02	0.03	0.08
Renfrewshire UA	0.03	0.04	0.04	0.11	-	0.04	0.01	0.05	0.16
Shetland Islands UA	0.02	0.15	0.03	0.19	-	0.05	0.06	0.11	0.30
South Ayrshire UA	0.01	0.02	0.01	0.05	0.00	0.02	0.01	0.03	0.07
South Lanarkshire UA	0.02	0.21	0.03	0.25	-	0.08	0.07	0.15	0.40
Stirling UA	0.00	0.04	-	0.04	0.00	0.06	0.01	0.07	0.11
West Lothian UA	0.02	0.24	0.20	0.45	0.01	0.06	0.05	0.12	0.57
Western Isles UA	-	0.01	0.03	0.04	0.00	-	0.01	0.01	0.05
Wales	0.23	1.96	0.66	2.85	0.02	0.74	0.52	1.27	4.12
Aberconwy & Colwyn UA	-	0.01	0.01	0.02	0.00	0.02	0.01	0.03	0.05
Anglesey UA	-	0.02	-	0.03	0.00	0.01	0.04	0.05	0.07
Blaenau Gwent UA	0.01	0.05	0.01	0.07	0.00	0.01	0.01	0.02	0.09
Bridgend UA	0.01	0.13	0.02	0.16	-	0.02	0.03	0.05	0.21
Caernarfonshire & Merionethshire UA	-	0.03	0.02	0.05	-	0.01	0.02	0.03	0.08
Caerphilly UA	0.03	0.04	0.04	0.11	-	0.04	0.01	0.05	0.16
Cardiff UA	0.02	0.15	0.03	0.19	-	0.05	0.06	0.11	0.30
Cardiganshire UA	0.01	0.02	0.01	0.05	0.00	0.02	0.01	0.03	0.07
Carmarthenshire UA	0.02	0.21	0.03	0.25	-	0.08	0.07	0.15	0.40
Denbighshire UA	0.00	0.04	-	0.04	0.00	0.06	0.01	0.07	0.11
Flintshire UA	0.02	0.24	0.20	0.45	0.01	0.06	0.05	0.12	0.57
Merthyr Tydfil UA	-	0.01	0.03	0.04	0.00	-	0.01	0.01	0.05
Monmouthshire UA	-	0.07	0.07	0.14	0.00	0.01	0.01	0.02	0.16
Neath & Port Talbot UA	-	0.06	0.02	0.09	0.00	0.02	0.02	0.04	0.13
Newport UA	0.02	0.30	0.02	0.35	-	0.08	0.02	0.10	0.45
Pembrokeshire UA	-	0.09	0.01	0.10	0.00	0.05	0.03	0.08	0.18
Powys UA	0.03	0.11	0.04	0.18	0.00	0.07	0.03	0.10	0.28
Rhondda, Cynon, Taff UA	0.02	0.12	0.03	0.18	0.00	0.02	0.02	0.04	0.21
Swansea UA	-	0.05	0.02	0.07	0.00	0.04	0.03	0.07	0.14
Torfaen UA	0.01	0.03	0.01	0.05	0.00	0.02	-	0.02	0.07
The Vale of Glamorgan UA	-	0.10	0.01	0.12	-	0.03	0.03	0.06	0.18
Wrexham UA	0.01	0.08	0.03	0.13	-	0.02	0.03	0.05	0.18

Table 21 (Cont'd)

Country/region/local authority	Rigid vehicles				All goods vehicles
	2 axle	3 axle	4 axle	All	
West Midland Region	33.80	3.79	2.07	39.66	51.47
Hereford & Worcestershire	3.49	0.43	0.16	4.08	5.56
Salop	2.40	0.33	0.22	2.95	4.03
Staffordshire	6.25	0.67	0.52	7.45	10.71
Warwickshire	2.54	0.29	0.21	3.04	4.05
West Midlands	19.12	2.06	0.96	22.15	27.12
North Western Region	35.71	3.19	2.20	41.10	55.42
Cheshire	4.82	0.56	0.38	5.76	8.94
Greater Manchester	19.58	1.49	0.80	21.87	27.64
Lancashire	7.55	0.73	0.54	8.83	11.87
Merseyside	3.75	0.41	0.48	4.65	6.97
Scotland	0.18	0.03	0.02	0.22	0.30
Aberdeen City UA	1.62	0.17	0.05	1.84	2.14
Aberdeenshire UA	0.49	0.09	0.08	0.65	1.06
Angus UA	0.89	0.17	0.11	1.18	1.57
Argyll & Bute UA	2.91	0.24	0.05	3.20	3.70
The Scottish Borders UA	0.91	0.21	0.07	1.19	1.55
Clackmannanshire UA	0.13	0.01	0.01	0.15	0.18
West Dunbartonshire UA	0.20	0.04	0.02	0.27	0.34
Dumfries & Galloway UA	0.29	0.06	0.04	0.39	0.60
City of Dundee UA	0.38	0.05	0.02	0.45	0.57
East Ayrshire UA	1.32	0.18	0.21	1.71	2.39
East Dunbartonshire UA	0.14	0.05	0.01	0.19	0.22
East Lothian UA	0.47	0.11	0.03	0.61	0.82
East Renfrewshire UA	0.47	0.14	0.11	0.71	1.06
City of Endinburgh UA	0.16	0.03	0.01	0.20	0.23
Falkirk UA	0.40	0.06	0.05	0.51	0.70
Fife UA	1.04	0.13	0.12	1.28	1.63
City of Glasgow UA	0.65	0.07	0.04	0.76	0.89
Highland UA	0.76	0.12	0.05	0.93	1.26
Inverclyde UA	0.15	0.04	0.01	0.20	0.25
Midlothian UA	11.72	1.43	0.98	14.13	18.25
Moray UA	0.38	0.03	0.07	0.48	0.53
North Ayrshire UA	0.30	0.04	0.01	0.35	0.42
North Lanarkshire UA	0.14	0.01	0.01	0.16	0.25
Orkney Islands UA	0.40	0.03	0.06	0.48	0.69
Perth & Kinross UA	0.58	0.06	0.04	0.68	0.76
Renfrewshire UA	0.53	0.05	0.05	0.63	0.79
Shetland Islands UA	1.42	0.07	0.06	1.55	1.85
South Ayrshire UA	0.40	0.04	0.01	0.45	0.52
South Lanarkshire UA	0.96	0.16	0.07	1.18	1.58
Stirling UA	0.40	0.06	0.06	0.52	0.63
West Lothian UA	0.71	0.10	0.13	0.95	1.51
Western Isles UA	0.17	0.01	0.01	0.18	0.23
Wales	11.72	1.43	0.98	14.13	18.25
Aberconwy & Colwyn UA	0.38	0.03	0.07	0.48	0.53
Anglesey UA	0.30	0.04	0.01	0.35	0.42
Blaenau Gwent UA	0.14	0.01	0.01	0.16	0.25
Bridgend UA	0.40	0.03	0.06	0.48	0.69
Caernarfonshire & Merionethshire UA	0.58	0.06	0.04	0.68	0.76
Caerphilly UA	0.53	0.05	0.05	0.63	0.79
Cardiff UA	1.42	0.07	0.06	1.55	1.85
Cardiganshire UA	0.40	0.04	0.01	0.45	0.52
Carmarthenshire UA	0.96	0.16	0.07	1.18	1.58
Denbighshire UA	0.40	0.06	0.06	0.52	0.63
Flintshire UA	0.71	0.10	0.13	0.95	1.51
Merthyr Tydfil UA	0.17	0.01	0.01	0.18	0.23
Monmouthshire UA	0.41	0.04	0.02	0.47	0.63
Neath & Port Talbot UA	0.34	0.04	0.03	0.41	0.53
Newport UA	0.83	0.10	0.06	0.99	1.43
Pembrokeshire UA	0.48	0.09	0.04	0.61	0.78
Powys UA	1.00	0.22	0.09	1.32	1.59
Rhondda, Cynon, Taff UA	0.72	0.10	0.09	0.91	1.12
Swansea UA	0.67	0.04	0.02	0.73	0.87
Torfaen UA	0.22	0.01	-	0.23	0.30
The Vale of Glamorgan UA	0.26	0.07	0.03	0.36	0.55
Wrexham UA	0.41	0.06	0.03	0.51	0.68

Table 22 Goods vehicle stock at end of year: 1986 -1996: by year of 1st registration

Thousands

Rigid vehicles

Year of 1st registration	1986	1987	1988	1989	1990	1991	1992	1993	1994	1995	1996
Pre 1978	54.0										
1978	23.6	61.6	71.4								
1979	35.4	30.3		73.8	62.9						
1980	32.3	28.7	24.1			57.6	57.9				
1981	26.2	24.2	21.4	18.4				63.7	71.0		
1982	27.7	26.3	24.4	21.7	17.5					73.0	81.4
1983	32.1	31.3	29.7	27.4	23.4	19.4					
1984	34.6	34.1	33.1	30.9	27.4	23.5	20.5				
1985	36.4	36.1	35.2	33.9	31.2	28.1	25.1	22.4			
1986	38.8	36.4	35.8	34.7	33.2	30.5	28.0	25.4	22.8		
1987		37.6	37.8	37.3	35.9	34.2	32.2	30.4	28.3	24.0	
1988			44.0	44.5	43.1	41.5	39.8	38.1	36.0	33.3	29.9
1989				45.1	44.8	43.4	42.2	41.2	39.3	36.6	33.5
1990					33.8	31.6	31.2	30.8	29.7	28.2	26.0
1991						20.0	20.2	20.2	19.6	19.3	17.8
1992							19.1	19.7	19.2	18.9	18.0
1993								20.6	21.1	21.1	20.4
1994									25.5	26.3	25.7
1995										29.8	30.0
1996											28.4
All years	341.1	346.5	357.0	367.6	353.3	329.9	316.2	312.5	312.4	310.5	311.0

Articulated vehicles

Year of 1st registration	1986	1987	1988	1989	1990	1991	1992	1993	1994	1995	1996
Pre 1978	5.9										
1978	5.8	8.7	11.5								
1979	9.3	7.7		11.5	9.4						
1980	7.8	6.6	5.2			8.9	9.5				
1981	7.0	6.2	5.2	3.9				10.8	13.2		
1982	9.0	8.3	7.4	6.1	4.4					13.6	14.9
1983	10.3	9.9	9.1	7.8	6.0	4.4					
1984	11.7	11.5	11.0	10.1	8.4	6.7	5.6				
1985	12.8	12.7	12.3	11.7	10.5	8.7	7.5	6.0			
1986	13.7	12.6	12.4	11.8	11.0	9.7	8.6	7.1	6.1		
1987		13.9	14.0	13.6	12.8	11.9	11.0	9.7	8.6	6.7	
1988			16.7	16.7	16.2	15.4	14.6	13.3	12.4	10.6	8.7
1989				17.2	16.8	16.3	15.9	14.7	13.9	12.4	10.3
1990					11.1	10.2	10.1	9.5	9.2	8.4	7.3
1991						7.4	7.4	7.2	6.9	6.5	5.8
1992							8.5	8.4	8.1	7.6	7.0
1993								10.7	10.8	10.4	9.6
1994									14.0	14.0	13.5
1995										17.2	16.8
1996											15.8
All years	93.5	97.9	104.6	110.4	106.5	99.7	98.7	97.5	103.3	107.4	109.6

Rigid and articulated vehicles

Year of 1st registration	1986	1987	1988	1989	1990	1991	1992	1993	1994	1995	1996
Pre 1978	59.9										
1978	29.3	70.3	82.9								
1979	44.8	37.9		88.1	72.3						
1980	40.1	35.2	29.3			66.4	67.4				
1981	33.2	30.4	26.6	22.3				74.5	84.2		
1982	36.7	34.6	31.8	27.7	21.9					86.6	96.3
1983	42.4	41.2	38.8	35.2	29.4	23.9					
1984	46.4	45.5	44.0	41.0	35.8	30.3	26.0				
1985	49.2	48.7	47.5	45.5	41.7	36.8	32.6	28.5			
1986	52.5	48.9	48.2	46.5	44.2	40.2	36.6	32.6	28.8		
1987		51.4	51.7	50.9	48.7	46.1	43.2	40.2	36.9	30.7	
1988			60.7	61.2	59.3	56.9	54.4	51.4	48.4	43.9	38.6
1989				62.3	61.6	59.8	58.1	55.9	53.2	49.0	43.8
1990					44.8	41.8	41.3	40.3	38.9	36.6	33.2
1991						27.4	27.6	27.4	26.5	25.7	23.6
1992							27.6	28.0	27.4	26.5	25.0
1993								31.3	31.9	31.5	29.9
1994									39.5	40.3	39.2
1995										47.1	46.8
1996											44.2
All years	434.6	444.4	461.6	478.0	459.7	429.6	414.9	410.1	415.7	418.0	420.6

Table 23 Goods vehicle stock at end of year: 1986 -1996: by gross vehicle weight

Thousands

Over	Not over	1986	1987	1988	1989	1990	1991	1992	1993	1994	1995	1996
Rigid vehicles												
3.5 t	7.5 t	150.8	155.0	161.9	169.5	166.2	157.8	152.0	151.4	150.2	150.8	153.3
7.5 t	12 t	26.4	24.9	23.3	22.0	20.1	18.5	17.2	16.6	15.9	16.0	15.7
12 t	16 t	39.2	36.7	34.5	32.2	29.2	26.0	24.3	23.5	22.7	23.1	22.2
16 t	20 t	80.1	82.8	86.7	89.9	87.1	80.9	77.9	75.6	75.7	74.0	73.1
20 t	24 t	1.0	1.4	1.8	2.1	2.4	2.5	2.7	3.0	3.4	3.9	4.7
24 t	28 t	25.6	26.2	27.2	28.3	26.6	24.5	23.3	23.2	24.0	23.4	23.6
28 t	32 t	17.9	19.4	21.6	23.5	21.5	19.5	18.6	18.5	19.9	19.1	18.4
32 t		0.1	0.1	0.1	0.2	0.2	0.2	0.2	0.6	0.6	0.0	0.0
All weights		341.1	346.5	357.0	367.6	353.3	329.9	316.2	312.5	312.4	310.5	311.0
Articulated vehicles												
3.5 t	16 t	0.6	0.5	0.5	0.5	0.5	0.4	0.3	0.3	0.3	0.4	0.3
16 t	20 t	4.1	3.7	3.1	2.8	2.4	2.1	1.9	1.7	1.5	1.4	1.3
20 t	24 t	1.1	1.1	1.1	1.0	1.1	1.0	1.1	1.1	1.2	1.3	1.4
24 t	28 t	7.3	8.4	9.1	9.7	9.7	9.2	9.3	9.3	9.6	10.0	10.2
28 t	32 t	1.5	1.3	1.1	1.1	0.9	0.9	1.0	1.1	1.7	2.2	2.4
32 t	33 t	43.7	40.5	37.3	33.5	28.1	23.2	19.9	18.1	17.0	14.8	13.0
33 t	37 t	1.3	1.3	1.2	1.5	1.4	1.5	1.7	1.5	1.3	1.4	1.5
37 t	38 t	33.9	41.2	51.1	60.3	62.5	61.3	63.5	64.4	70.4	75.3	78.2
38 t		-	-	-	-	-	-	-	-	0.2	0.7	1.2
All weights		93.5	97.9	104.6	110.4	106.5	99.7	98.7	97.5	103.3	107.4	109.6
Rigid and articulated vehicles												
3.5 t	7.5 t	151.0	155.3	162.1	169.8	166.4	158.1	152.2	151.6	150.4	151.0	153.5
7.5 t	12 t	26.6	25.1	23.4	22.1	20.2	18.5	17.2	16.6	16.0	16.0	15.8
12 t	16 t	39.3	36.8	34.6	32.4	29.3	26.1	24.4	23.6	22.8	23.2	22.3
16 t	20 t	84.2	86.4	89.8	92.6	89.5	83.0	79.8	77.2	77.2	75.5	74.4
20 t	24 t	2.1	2.5	2.8	3.1	3.4	3.5	3.8	4.1	4.6	5.2	6.1
24 t	28 t	32.9	34.5	36.3	38.1	36.3	33.7	32.7	32.5	33.5	33.4	33.8
28 t	32 t	19.4	20.7	22.7	24.6	22.4	20.4	19.5	19.6	21.6	21.3	20.9
32 t	38 t	79.0	83.1	89.7	95.5	92.2	86.2	85.3	84.6	89.2	91.5	92.7
38 t		-	-	-	-	-	-	-	0.2	0.4	0.7	1.2
All weights		434.6	444.4	461.6	478.0	459.7	429.6	414.9	410.1	415.7	417.9	420.6

49

Table 24 Goods vehicles stock at end of year: 1991-1996: by gross vehicle weight, axle configuration

Thousands

Axles	Year	Over Not over	3.5 t 7.5 t	7.5 t 12 t	12 t 16 t	16 t 20 t	20 t 24 t	24 t 28 t	28 t 32 t	32 t 33 t	33 t 37 t	37 t 38 t	38 t	All weights
Rigid vehicles														
2 Axle	1991		160.3	18.5	26.7	79.1	0.1	0.3	0.2	-	-	-	-	285.2
	1992		155.3	17.2	25.0	76.9	0.1	0.3	0.2	-	-	-	-	275.0
	1993		151.3	16.6	23.5	75.4	0.1	0.2	0.2	0.2	0.3	-	0.2	268.0
	1994		150.1	15.9	22.6	75.3	0.1	0.2	0.1	0.2	0.2	0.0	0.2	264.9
	1995		150.7	15.9	22.8	73.5	-	-	-	-	0.0	-	-	263.1
	1996		153.1	15.7	21.9	72.6	-	0.0	0.0	-	0.0	0.0	0.0	263.2
3 Axles	1991		0.1	-	0.1	0.3	2.4	23.5	-	-	-	-	-	26.4
	1992		0.1	-	-	0.2	2.7	22.9	-	-	-	-	-	26.0
	1993		0.1	-	-	0.2	2.9	22.8	-	-	-	-	-	26.1
	1994		0.1	0.0	0.0	0.4	3.3	23.6	0.0	0.0	0.0	0.0	0.0	27.5
	1995		0.1	0.1	0.1	0.4	3.9	23.3	0.0	-	0.0	-	0.0	27.8
	1996		0.1	0.1	0.1	0.4	4.6	23.5	0.0	0.0	0.0	0.0	0.0	28.8
4 Axles	1991		-	-	-	-	-	0.2	18.6	-	-	-	-	18.8
	1992		-	-	-	-	-	0.2	18.3	-	-	-	-	18.5
	1993		-	-	-	-	-	0.1	18.3	-	-	-	-	18.5
	1994		0.0	0.0	0.0	0.0	0.0	0.2	19.7	0.0	0.0	0.0	0.0	20.0
	1995		-	-	0.2	0.1	-	0.1	19.1	-	0.0	0.0	0.0	19.6
	1996		0.1	-	0.2	0.1	-	0.1	18.4	0.0	0.0	0.0	0.0	18.9
All	1991		160.4	18.6	26.8	79.3	2.6	24.0	18.8	-	-	-	-	330.5
	1992		155.4	17.3	25.0	77.1	2.8	23.4	18.5	-	-	-	-	319.5
	1993		151.4	16.6	23.5	75.6	3.0	23.2	18.5	0.2	0.3	-	0.2	312.5
	1994		150.2	15.9	22.7	75.7	3.4	24.0	19.9	0.2	0.2	0.0	0.2	312.4
	1995		150.8	16.0	23.1	74.0	3.9	23.4	19.1	-	0.0	-	-	310.5
	1996		153.3	15.7	22.2	73.1	4.7	23.6	18.4	-	0.0	0.0	0.0	311.0
Articulated vehicles														
2 Axle	1991			0.4		2.0	1.0	8.8	0.7	21.3	1.3	33.5	-	69.0
tractive	1992			0.3		1.8	1.0	8.8	0.9	18.4	1.5	34.8	-	67.5
units	1993			0.3		1.7	1.1	9.1	1.1	17.7	1.3	35.9	-	68.3
	1994		0.2	0.0	0.1	1.5	1.2	9.4	1.7	16.6	1.1	39.2	0.0	71.0
	1995		0.2	-	0.1	1.4	1.2	9.6	2.1	14.2	1.2	42.2	-	72.3
	1996		0.2	-	-	1.3	1.3	9.7	2.4	12.5	1.3	44.2	-	72.9
3 Axles	1991			-		-	-	0.1	-	0.3	0.2	25.1	-	25.7
tractive	1992			-		-	-	0.2	-	0.3	0.2	26.7	-	27.3
units	1993			-		-	-	0.2	-	0.4	0.2	28.5	-	29.3
	1994		0.0	0.0	0.0	0.0	0.0	0.1	0.0	0.4	0.2	31.2	0.2	32.3
	1995		-	-	-	0.1	-	0.3	0.1	0.5	0.2	33.1	0.7	35.1
	1996		0.1	-	-	0.1	0.1	0.5	0.1	0.5	0.2	34.0	1.2	36.8
All	1991			0.4		2.0	1.0	8.9	0.7	21.6	1.5	58.6	-	94.7
	1992			0.3		1.9	1.0	8.9	0.9	18.6	1.6	61.5	-	94.8
	1993			0.3		1.7	1.1	9.3	1.1	18.1	1.5	64.4	-	97.5
	1994		0.2	0.0	0.1	1.5	1.2	9.6	1.7	17.0	1.3	70.4	0.2	103.3
	1995		0.2	0.1	0.1	1.4	1.3	10.0	2.2	14.8	1.4	75.3	0.7	107.4
	1996		0.2	-	0.1	1.3	1.4	10.2	2.4	13.0	1.5	78.2	1.2	109.6

Notes and Definitions

1. NOTES ON THE VEHICLE INFORMATION DATABASE

1.1 Most of the information in this publication is drawn from a Vehicle Information Database (VID), held in the Department of Transport's Statistics Directorate and updated quarterly using information supplied by DVLA. The results conform to the same definitions as earlier vehicle censuses, but, for technical reasons, are considered slightly more reliable than earlier estimates.

1.2 Some vehicles have complicated licensing histories, that may include incidents such as cheques failing to clear, changes of taxation status, late payments, and one or more valid or invalid refund claims. The VID undertakes a more detailed examination of licensing history than earlier vehicle census analyses and is therefore able to provide better estimates of licensed stock.

2. NOTES ON CURRENTLY LICENSED STOCK STATISTICS: TABLES 1 to 8

Effects of using the Vehicle Information Database

2.1 The net effect of the change to the VID as the main source of statistics on currently licensed stock was to produce a small reduction - of the order of 1% - in the estimated levels of licensed stock. A number of main tables showing time series of licensed stock have therefore been broken at 1992, and show both the series based on previous census analyses up to 1992, and a series from 1992 taken from the VID. Estimates of changes between years before and after 1992 can be made by combining the changes from the two series.

Census methods used in earlier publications

2.2 Censuses based entirely on the record of licensed vehicles at DVLA began on 31 December 1978, and subsequent counts have been taken on the last day of the year up to and including 31st December 1992. There are two important differences between the censuses based entirely on DVLA records and censuses prior to 1978.

2.4 Firstly, censuses derived from DVLA records were based on a single point (one day) in time. In previous censuses, for purely administrative reasons, counts of licensed vehicles at Local Taxation Offices included any vehicle licensed for at least one month during the third quarter of the year.

2.5 Secondly, the DVLA-based censuses relied on a complete count of all vehicles, subject only to the complexities of establishing accurately the licensing status of the vehicle, whereas before 1978, information on vehicle stock had been obtained from samples.

Taxation class changes

2.6 There have been three major changes in recent years. Firstly, as from 1 October 1982, all general goods vehicles less than 1,525 kgs unladen weight were assessed for vehicle excise duty at the same rate as private vehicles, and the old "private car and van" taxation class was replaced by the new "Private and Light Goods" (PLG) taxation class. In addition, goods vehicles greater than 1,525 kgs unladen weight were to be taxed with reference to their gross vehicle weight and axle configuration, as opposed to unladen weight as in previous years. Farmers' light goods vehicles and showmen's light goods vehicles, i.e. vehicles of less than 1,525 kgs unladen weight, were allocated to their own distinct taxation classes and were not included in the PLG taxation class.

2.7 Secondly, from 1 October 1990, goods vehicles less than 3,500 kgs gross vehicle weight were transferred from the "Goods Vehicle" taxation class to the "Private and Light Goods" class. Farmers' and showmen's goods vehicles of less than 3,500 kgs gross vehicle weight, but more than 1,525 kgs unladen weight, were transferred to the "Light Goods Farmers' and "Light Goods Showmen's" taxation classes.

2.8 Finally 1995 saw major reforms of the vehicle taxation system. The bulk of the 1995 changes came into operation on 1st July 1995, but some additional changes were introduced on 29th November 1995. The intention was to remove many of the complications in the existing taxation structure, using a strategy to link VED rates for many directly to the rate for the private and light goods group (PLG), or the basic minimum rate for heavy goods vehicles (HGVs). One measure to help achieve this was the creation of three "umbrella" taxation groups:-

An emergency vehicles group - exempt from VED.

A special concessionary group, including agricultural machines, snow ploughs, gritting vehicles, electric vehicles and, later, steam powered vehicles, paying VED, at current rates, of £35 per annum, or one quarter of the annal PLG rate.

A special vehicles group, limited to vehicles over 3500 kgs, including mobile cranes, works trucks, digging machines, showmen's vehicles, etc., paying VED at a rate equivalent to the basic minimum rate for HGVs, currently £150.

2.9 In addition, the goods vehicle taxation system was itself considerably simplified by the abolition of separate goods vehicle classes for farmers and showmen. All remaining light goods vehicle taxation classes were also abolished and vehicles in those groups transferred to the PLG class. At the same time, the basis for calculation of excise duty for goods vehicles was amended to "revenue weight". Revenue weight means either "confirmed maximum gross weight" as determined by plating and testing regulations, or "design weight" for vehicles not subject to plating and testing (formerly known as Restricted HGVs).

2.10 The process also included further simplifications and "tidying" arrangements. These included cases in which vehicles not over less than 3500 kgs gross weight were moved into the private and light goods taxation class rather than remaining in specialised taxation classes and groups, and the re-allocation of some tax classes into more appropriate groups. One key change of a similar type was to abolish the separate taxation of public transport vehicles with eight seats of fewer and tax all such vehicles in the PLG class. From start of July 1995 bigger public transport vehicles were taxed in a new "bus taxation class. The changes were completed by the introduction of a new exempt class in the November 1995 budget for vehicles previously in the private and light goods or motorcycle groups over 25 of years of age.

2.11 In general, the process of implementing these changes was gradual, and vehicles were allowed to remain in their current class until a new tax disk was required, whereupon they were transferred into other groups and classes as appropriate. Since tax disks may run for up to a year, some vehicles remained legitimately taxed in abolished groups at the end of 1995. That process was effectively complete by the end of 1996, but users of taxation and stock statistics for 1995 and 1996 should take special care to ensure they are aware of the changes and the methods by which vehicles were re-allocated to other groups.

Correction for taxation class changes

2.12 The changes described above created discontinuities in the time series for vehicles currently licensed. To correct for these discontinuities, retrospective estimates of "Private and Light Goods" and "Goods" have been made for the years before 1991 using the assumption that all general goods vehicles of less than 3,500 kgs gross vehicle weight would have been taxed as "Private and Light Goods". Private cars taxed within "Private and Light Goods" have been estimated pro-rata on the basis of information on the proportion of cars within "Private and Light Goods" available for the first time in 1983.

2.13 Between 1978 and 1982, the distribution of private cars, within "Private and Light Goods", by engine capacity has been estimated pro-rata by allocating retrospective estimates for total private cars within "Private and Light Goods" across previous distributions of "private cars and vans" by engine capacity.

2.14 As described in paragraph 2.6 above, since October 1982 gross vehicle weight has been the basis of taxation for goods vehicles. Analyses of the stock of goods vehicles by gross weight have been compiled since the 1983 census. Pre-1983 time series analysed by gross vehicle weight are not available.

2.15 Although the 1995 changes will have an influence on the number of vehicles taxed within the PLG group, the effects are small compared to the large number of vehicles in that group, and the PLG series has not been subject to any retrospective adjustment or recalculation. Retrospective series have been estimated for the new "bus" taxation class and are included in the tables.

Regional analysis

2.16 The only regional information easily obtainable from vehicle records held on computer by DVLA is the post code of the registered keeper of the vehicle. Until 1995 this information was used by DVLA to allocate the vehicle to the county in which the registered keeper lived. County and regional analyses in all previous edditions of Vehicle Licensing Statistics were compiled in this way. Vehicles under disposal are those where the previous owner has sold the vehicle and notified DVLA, but the new keeper has not completed and returned his part of the registration document. For such vehicles the post code of the registered keeper is unknown.

2.17 With the 1996 re-organisation of local authorities in Scotland and Wales, and the creation of new unitary authorities in some parts of England regional analyses required major revisions. This was acheived by use of the most recently available post code directory, which, when used in conjunction with the vehicle information datbase, allowed vehicle stocks to be estimated for the new local authorities in Scotland and Wales, and for those unitary authorites that have been created so far in England. Similar changes have been made in Table 24, which deals with goods vehicle stocks by region.

3. NOTES ON VEHICLES REGISTERED FOR THE 1ST TIME: TABLES 10 to 13

Sources

3.1 The statistics in this section are based on a complete analysis of new registrations and not on a sample count. Monthly analyses are compiled from the records of the Driver and Vehicle Licensing Agency (DVLA) by its Information Technology contractor, and forwarded to the Department of Transport's Statistics Directorate.

Correction for taxation class changes

3.2 To correct for taxation class changes, as described under sections 2.6 and 2.7 above, retrospective estimates of "Private and Light Goods" and "General Goods" were made for 1969 to 1982 by assuming that all "general goods" vehicles less than 1,525 kgs unladen vehicle weight would have been registered as PLG prior to 1 October 1982, if that taxation class had been in operation. A second set of retrospective estimates was made for 1980 to 1990 assuming that general goods vehicles of less than 3,500 kgs gross weight would have been registered as PLG.

3.3 From 1975 onwards, estimates have been made of the number of private cars taxed within the "Private and Light Goods" class. Up to 1982 general goods vehicles and Farmers' goods were taxed on their unladen weight and analyses were produced on this basis. Since 1983 gross vehicle weight has been the basis of taxation and new registrations have been analysed by gross vehicle weight.

3.4 Changes to the vehicle taxation system in 1995 will see vehicles register under the new structure from 1st July 1995. Future publications will reflect these changes and some time series will contain unavoidable discontinuities. However, time series for some individual tax classes may still be available even where the calls has been allocated to a different taxation group. For example, agricultural tractors, previously part of the "agricultural and special machines" group, now fall into the "special concessionary" group. See table 11.

4. NOTES ON HISTORIC SERIES: TABLES 9 AND 14

Motor vehicles currently licensed: census methods

4.1 Up to 1974, the figures for motor vehicles currently licensed were compiled from information received by the Department of Transport from all registration/licensing authorities or Local Taxation Offices (County, County Borough and Borough Councils) in Great Britain which administered the Vehicles (Excise) Act 1971.

4.2 Since October 1974, all new vehicles have been registered at the Driver and Vehicle Licensing Agency (DVLA), and records for older vehicles have also been transferred there, the process being completed in March 1978. For 1975 and 1976 the census was based on a combination of records held at Local Taxation Offices and at DVLA. Because of the closure of Local Taxation Offices it was not possible to produce census results in 1977. This system was superseded by censuses based entirely on the record of licensed vehicles at DVLA on 31 December 1978. Differences between censuses based entirely on DVLA records and those prior to 1978 are described in sections 3.4 and 3.5.

4.3 These differences produce a discontinuity in the stock figures in 1978. Pre-1978 figures have therefore been adjusted to make them comparable with those for later years. These adjustments have been applied after the estimation described under "correction for taxation class changes".

Correction for taxation class changes

4.4 The changes described above under 3.6 and 3.7 created a discontinuity in the time series for vehicles currently licensed. To correct for this discontinuity, retrospective estimates of "Private and Light Goods" and "Goods" have been made for the years 1950 to 1982, using the assumption that all general goods vehicles of less than 3,500 kgs gross vehicle weight would have been taxed as "Private and Light Goods" if this class had existed prior to 1983. Private cars taxed within "Private and Light Goods" have been estimated pro-rata on the basis of information on the proportion of cars within "Private and Light Goods" available for the first time in 1983.

4.5 The "Goods" category retains Farmers' goods vehicles and showmen's goods vehicles of less than 1,525 kgs unladen weight. From 1983, retrospective counts of vehicles within the new taxation class groupings were produced. Other taxation classes were unaffected by the change in goods vehicle taxation.

Motor vehicles registered for the first time

4.6 Statistics in this table are based on a complete analysis of new registrations and not on a sample count. In the past these were obtained from monthly returns of licensing authorities' records of new registrations. On 1 October 1974 the Driver and Vehicle Licensing Centre (DVLC) at Swansea took over responsibility for the licensing of vehicles from Local Taxation Offices (LTO). Initially, DVLC dealt only with new registrations, but from 1 April 1975 they began to take on the registration of older vehicles from the Local Vehicle Licensing Offices, which replaced the LTOs. On 1 April 1990, DVLC became the Driver and Vehicle Licensing Agency (DVLA).

Correction for taxation class changes

4.7 To correct for taxation class changes, retrospective estimates of "Private and Light Goods" and "General Goods" have been made for 1951 to 1982 by assuming that all "general goods" vehicles less than 3,500 kgs gross vehicle weight would have been registered as "Private and Light Goods" prior to 1 October 1982, if that taxation class had been in operation. The "Goods Vehicles" taxation class retains Farmers' goods vehicles and showmen's goods vehicles less than 1,525 kgs unladen weight. From 1975 onwards, estimates have been made of the number of private cars taxed within the "Private and Light Goods" class. Other taxation classes were unaffected by the change in goods vehicle taxation.

5.   NOTES ON GOODS VEHICLE STATISTICS: TABLES 15 TO 24

5.1 The purpose of tables 15 to 24 is to provide detailed information on heavy goods vehicles in terms of their GVW and axle configuration. This population of vehicles at the end of 1995 amounts to some 421,000 vehicles, compared with 413,000 vehicles in goods vehicle taxation groups. This difference reflects the inclusion of some goods vehicles in electric and exempt taxation classes in the former group and the abolition of specialised goods taxation classes containing vehicles not more than 3500 kgs gross weight in the latter.

Goods vehicles statistics in this publication

5.2 The goods vehicle statistics provided in tables 15 onwards cover those goods vehicles over 3.5 tonnes gross vehicle weight (GVW), in taxation groups 1 and 2, that is HGV, trailer HGV and class 16 small island goods vehicles. In addition, results include vehicles in electric taxation class, crown vehicles, and vehicles with various forms of exemption, provided they exceed 3.5 tonnes gross vehicle weight have goods vehicle body type and comply with appropriate axle and weight limit regulations. Further information on taxation groups is given in table 3.

Goods vehicle statistics in earlier publications

5.3 Previous publications of "Goods Vehicles In Great Britain" were based primarily on results taken from the Goods Vehicle List (GVL), a register of vehicles over 3.5 tonnes gross weight licensed to carry goods on the public road network, and maintained by the DVLA. This list is a count of goods vehicles (greater than 3.5 tonnes gross weight) designed to provide a sampling population for the Continuing Survey of Road Goods Transport (CSRGT). However, some tables in that publication were drawn from the "Goods Vehicle Census", as described below.

5.4 Following the Armitage inquiry, the maximum weight limit for articulated vehicles was increased from 32.5 tonnes gross vehicle weight (GVW) to 38 tonnes GVW, effective from 1 May 1983. To monitor the effect of this change the Goods Vehicle Census, a new source of information on goods vehicles greater than 3.5 tonnes GVW and 1,525 kgs unladen weight (ULW), was developed based on the DVLA register. It was designed to produce detailed information on heavy goods vehicles in terms of their GVW and axle configuration. This census included goods vehicles in a wider range of tax classes than the Goods Vehicle List, including certain goods vehicles in exempt classes.

5.5 Earlier editions of "Goods Vehicles In Great Britain" explained how it was possible to reconcile the alternative estimates of goods vehicle stock provided by the two sources. After allowing for the differences in coverage the two estimates are close, the differences being attributable to the timing of the counts. The Goods Vehicle Census is taken six weeks after the end of the year census day to allow for the processing lag between application for licence and entry into the register. The GVL counts are taken on the last day of each calendar quarter since timely counts are needed for the CSRGT. Because of its use in sampling active vehicles the GVL contains recently unlicensed vehicles which may be in the process of relicensing.

6. TAXATION CLASS DEFINITIONS

Exempt vehicles

6.1 The exempt vehicles includes a number of distinct sub-groups and classes, of which the most important are emergency vehicles, crown vehicles, disabled driver and disabled passenger carrying vehicles, vehicles previously taxed in PLG, motorcycle or tricycle tax groups but over 25 years of age and personal export and direct export vehicles. Most exempt vehicle classes required to obtain and display an annual tax disk but pay a nil rate of duty.

6.2 Vehicles owned by Government Departments and operated under Certificates of Crown ownership (apart from those belonging to the Armed Forces) are registered but exempt from vehicle excise duty. The exempt vehicle statistics exclude cars and motor cycles used temporarily in Great Britain before being privately exported under the personal export and direct export schemes by non-United Kingdom citizens.

General haulage

6.4 General haulage vehicles may not be used for carrying loads or transporting goods except on the trailer which it is towing, where, unlike articulated heavy goods vehicles, the trailer does not form an integral part of vehicles. Many vehicles taxed for general haulage are agricultural tractors.

Goods vehicles

6.5 Goods vehicles over 3,500 kgs gross vehicle weight. Now limited to two main groups, class 01 for heavy goods vehicles, and class 02 for goods vehicles paying additional trailer duty. Goods vehicles on certain off-shore islands may qualify to tax in class 16-small island goods.

Motorcycles, scooters and mopeds

6.6 No distinction between these different types of machine is made for taxation purposes. The vehicle excise duty payable depends upon the engine capacity of the bike.

Private and light goods

6.7 Includes all vehicles used privately. The bulk of this group consists of private cars (whether owned by individuals or companies) and vans and light goods vehicles. The group also contains a number of important minority groups including private buses and coaches, private heavy goods vehicles, and some vehicles which before 1st July 1995 were taxed in specialised taxation class but which do not exceed 3500 kgs gross weight and now fall into the PLG group. A substantial number of motorcars are now taxed in the exempt disabled driver class.

6.8 A new class "Private HGV" was introduced from 29th November 1995 for heavy goods vehicles used unladen, privately or for driver training purposes. The annual duty is a flat rate £150 the basic minimum rate for HGVs.

OXFORDSHIRE
COUNTY
LIBRARIES

Public transport vehicles

6.9 All vehicles classified for taxation purposes as class 34 - Bus. These are vehicles used for public conveyance, with more than 8 seats. Buses and coaches not licensed for public conveyance, and operated and used privately, are excluded and are classified for excise licensing with private and light goods. Taxis and private hire cars are now included in the private and light goods group and are not separately identified within the VED taxation system. Regulation and control of taxis and private hire cars is through local authorities who issue appropriate hackney and hire car plates.

Special concessionary group

6.10 This group of vehicles pays VED at the rate of £35 per annum and, in common with the former "agricultural and special machines" group includes agricultural tractors, combine harvesters and mowing machines. This taxation class also electric vehicles, gritting vehicles and snow ploughs, and steam powered vehicles. However, works trucks, mobile cranes and digging machines previously in the "agricultural and special machines" group are no longer included.

Special machines

6.11 This group consists of vehicles over 3500 kgs, which do not pay VED as heavy goods vehicles nor qualify for taxation in the special concessionary group. Vehicles in this group pay VED at the basic minimum rate for HGVs. Types include road rollers, works trucks and showman's vehicles.

Three wheelers

6.12 Mainly three-wheeled cars and vans not exceeding 450 kgs unladen weight. Motorised tricycles are also included but motorcycle combinations are included with motor cycles.

Trade licences

6.13 These are issued to manufacturers and repairers of, and dealers in, motor vehicles but as they do not relate to particular vehicles they are not included in any of the tables relating to current licences or new registrations.

Vehicles owned by the Armed Forces

6.14 Vehicles officially belonging to the Armed Forces, except for a small number which for particular reasons, are licensed in the ordinary way, operate under a special registration and licensing system operated by them. Such vehicles are excluded from vehicle registration figures.

Symbols and conventions

.. = not available	- = negligible (less than half the final digit shown)
0 = nil (that is exactly zero)	| = change or break in the series (cf. table 2)